WorkTips

ORGANIZING STRATEGIES FOR A PRODUCTIVE WORKLIFE

BY PATRICIA KATZ

The Seventh In The Best-Selling Series From The Publishers Of
Money and Time-Saving Household Hints
Environmental and Energy Household Hints
Getting It Together
A Year of Crafts
Cornerstones – An Artist's History of the City of Regina
HomeTips – Organizing Strategies for A Streamlined Home Life

Printed using vegetable-based (Canola) inks

Work*Tips*
by Patricia Katz

First Printing – January 1996

The Leader-Post Carrier Foundation Inc.
c/o The Leader-Post
1964 Park Street
P.O. Box 2020
Regina, Saskatchewan
Canada S4P 3G4

&

The Organizers
c/o Patricia Katz
315 O'Brien Place
Saskatoon, Saskatchewan
Canada S7K 6S9

Canadian Cataloguing in Publication Data

Katz, Patricia, 1952

Worktips

ISBN 1-895292-65-4

1. Time management. 2. Management. 3. Business
I. Leader-Post Carrier Foundation Inc. II. Title.

HD69.T54K389 1996 650.1 C95-920261-7

Cover and page design by
Yves Noblet

Author Photograph by
Stuart Kasdorf

Printed and Produced in Canada by
Centax Books, A Division of PrintWest Communications
Publishing Director – Margo Embury
1150 Eighth Avenue, Regina, Saskatchewan
Canada S4R 1C9
(306) 525-2304 Fax (306) 757-2439

LeaderPost
Carrier Foundation

The Leader-Post Carrier Foundation Inc. was established by Regina's daily newspaper as a tribute to its past and present carriers. Its aim is to support educational and humanitarian needs in Saskatchewan. While it is named in honor of carriers, help from the Foundation is available to the public at large.

Individual and corporate donations help fund the Foundation, but its primary income is from the proceeds of special projects organized on behalf of the Foundation by The Leader-Post.

Among the most successful projects have been previous books: *Money and Time-Saving Household Hints, Environmental and Energy Hints, Getting It Together, A Year of Crafts* and *Cornerstones, An Artist's History of The City of Regina. WorkTips: Organizing Strategies for a Productive Work Life* and *HomeTips: Organizing Strategies for a Streamlined Home Life*, are the Foundation's sixth and seventh publications. They are expanded, updated versions of Getting It Together, a sold-out success that has made a difference to the people who benefit from the Foundation's support.

The Organizers
PATRICIA KATZ

The Organizers, founded by Patricia Katz in 1986, provides information and inspiration to help individuals and organizations be more productive and effective.

As a speaker, trainer, author and consultant, Patricia is dedicated to researching and sharing practical ideas for managing complex lives.

Seminars and keynote presentations focus on: organization, time and stress management, as well as balancing work and family life.

Patricia is a CHRP (Certified Human Resource Professional), graduate Home Economist, and a member of the National Speakers Association and the National Association of Professional Organizers.

For further information, contact: Patricia Katz, The Organizers, 315 O'Brien Place, Saskatoon, SK, Canada, S7K 6S9. Ph: (306) 934-1807 Fax: (306) 242-0795 E-Mail: KatzP@sasknet.sk.ca

TABLE OF CONTENTS

PREFACE

Today's work place expectations are high. Fewer hands tackle larger workloads. Fax machines and electronic mail generate last minute requests for instant replies. This morning's developments shift this afternoon's priorities. The quantity of information in circulation is overwhelming; the quality is often uncertain. Technology offers shortcuts but learning time is limited.

Personal and professional success depends on our ability to organize our time, our ideas, our activities, and our surroundings in order to accomplish priority tasks and strengthen important relationships.

Good organizational skills are essential. They free us up to do the things that matter with the people who matter most in our lives – from clients and co-workers to family members and friends – with time and energy to care for our own needs, too!

Organizational skills are not a magic elixir. They will not solve every problem nor turn you into superman or superwoman. Even the highest degree of organization won't allow you to carry outrageous loads for endless periods of time without serious consequences. There are always choices to be made.

***WorkTips* is dedicated to my clients and colleagues for the challenges they present and the support they provide.**

Patricia Katz

The basic principles for getting organized, staying energized and living and working purposefully apply equally well in both our professional and personal lives.

* Take responsibility for influencing the events of your life
* Clarify your purpose
* Set goals to focus your action and be open to modifying your plans
* Balance "doing" and "being" to build both a record of achievement and a richness of relationship
* Sort priorities on a regular basis – solo and with others at work and at home
* Set up systems to handle recurring tasks
* Simplify and streamline the steps in every process
* Dejunk and unclutter life spaces as you go
* Choose organizing tools that fit your needs and learn to use them well
* Concentrate on the task at hand
* Take re-energizing renewing breaks
* Celebrate often

The contents of this book expand on these themes, offering concrete examples and suggestions.

Portions of this book previously appeared in an earlier publication, *Getting It Together*, which combined information on both work and family life. The original material has been divided in two and multiplied by two (supplemented with brand-new material) to bring you these expanded volumes, each with their own focus.

WorkTips focuses on the challenges of paid work – careers, jobs, and businesses. It presents organizing strategies for a more productive work life.

HomeTips, the companion volume, focuses on the world of unpaid work – our personal and family lives. It offers organizing strategies for a more streamlined home life.

I invite you to explore both books and am certain you will find these ideas of value.

Remember that knowing about an idea and putting it into practice are two different things. Testing and applying these techniques is what will make a difference in your life.

Good luck and good living!

"Talk does not cook rice!"

Chinese Proverb

THE BIG PICTURE

I CAN SEE CLEARLY NOW

It doesn't matter how fast or efficiently you can get things done – if you're working on the wrong thing, you're wasting your time.

Many of the concerns related to organization and time management have to do with getting everything done in less time rather than making sure the important things are handled.

It's understandable. Struggling to sort out the larger purpose and direction is hard work. Sorting paper and projects in progress is easy in comparison.

Addressing the questions of purpose, value and direction takes large chunks of uninterrupted time and leads directly to conflicting desires and destinations. Resolving these conflicts is not easy.

However, the payback is immense. When the big questions are answered, the small ones are easy.

For renewing energy and commitment, there is nothing more powerful than a retreat from daily action. You may be able to address these questions on your own or with colleagues or you may need the help of an outside facilitator to lead you through the process.

The objective is to clarify the long-range purpose and mission of your business or organization. In the largest possible sense, what is it that you are trying to accomplish? In what arena? With what impact?

A clear vision (the big picture) then needs to be translated into a set of objectives for the short term. What are your specific targets for the coming year? Where do they rank in order of importance?

Sharing thoughts on how you will work together is just as critical as addressing what you will tackle. Take time to discuss how you will organize yourselves to communicate, make further decisions, address problems, support each other and celebrate your successes.

Maps that are created and then tucked away in a bottom drawer do nothing to guide a journey. Find ways to keep your plans visible. Post progress charts, reminders and images of your goals and targets.

Build in checkpoints by blocking out refocus sessions throughout the year. Set aside time every few months during the year to review the big picture, check progress and problem-solve obstacles. Set dates for the refocus sessions for the entire year so they are on record right from the start.

Create time policies that support your goals. Think in terms of minimums, maximums, annual choices and targets.

Block out a minimum of x hours per week on your calendar for High Priority Project X. Note your commitment before the time gets chewed up by lesser priorities.

Set maximum limits on involvements that are likely to pull you off course. While you pursue other priorities, you may choose to limit your volunteer involvement in community or professional associations to one executive position at a time.

Make annual choices. Decide which charities you will support during the next twelve months. You'll find it more straightforward and less time consuming than to respond to donation requests through the year.

Choose a recurring job function and track how long it takes you to finish it each time. Benchmark the task to see how long it takes others to accomplish the same task. Aim to meet or better the shortest time.

When you are clear about what it is you want to make happen, committed to that vision, specific in your targets and deadlines, you will find ways to move in your direction of choice.

"Learn enough about your goal that you would recognize it if you saw it."

Robert Fritz

THE BIG PICTURE

LIGHTEN THE LOAD

Raise your hands now. How many of you woke up this morning feeling like you had been run over by a Mac truck? Overwhelmed before you even lifted those lids? Knowing that you've got tons of things to do, and that most of them should have been done yesterday?

It's tough to move when you're burdened by the weight of the world.

Working with a world-class backup of "things to do" is like wading through soft sand, deep water or three feet of snow. You can't get up to speed and even when you're moving, it feels like you're not getting anywhere. You're still buried ... swamped ... snowed under.

You need to set priorities to lighten the daily load. Picture it this way.

Shuttling between your home and office is a semitrailer unit with your name painted on the side. You are constantly loading it with tasks that need your attention and with ideas for how to spend your time. Family members, colleagues and supervisors, friends and neighbors know the combination on the lock and are also tossing things in your trailer.

If you carry, tow or drive that loaded semi everywhere you go, you'll move more slowly, be less effective and feel like you're beat before you start.

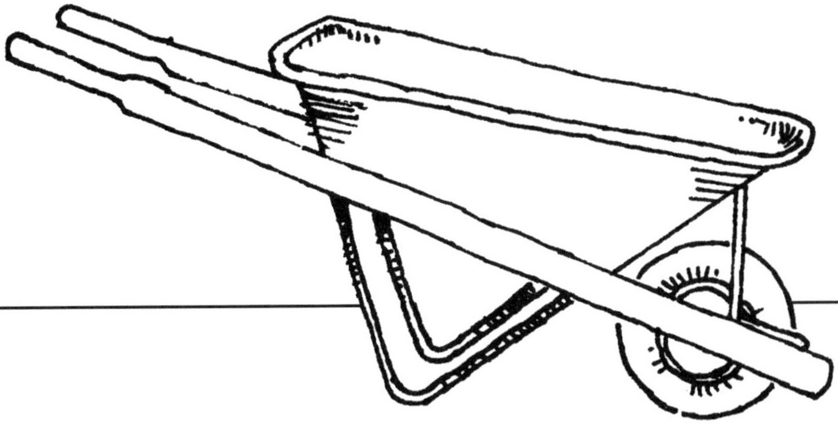

Do this instead. At the beginning of every month, back your half-ton truck up to the semi. Open the doors on the trailer, jump inside and take a look around. Ask yourself: "What are the most valuable things for me to accomplish over the next thirty days – for my work, my family, my community and myself?" Consider both the urgency and importance of the tasks.

Haul out those tasks. Load them in the half-ton truck and close the doors on the semi. Park the smaller truck in your driveway.

At the beginning of every week – sometime on Sunday – roll your wheelbarrow over to the half ton truck. Ask yourself: "Of this month's priorities, what are the most important things to be tackled in the next seven days for my work, my family, my community and myself?" Load up those tasks.

Take a close look at the size of the load. Can you handle it? Do you need to delay anything – toss a few items back in the half-ton? Do you need to delegate or look for help with certain tasks? Do you need to drop something completely?

Few of us work or live in isolation. You'll need to discuss the contents of the load and compare plans for the week with family members and business partners.

Take the required action and park the wheelbarrow in your garage. Now, each morning when the alarm goes off, you need only concern yourself with choosing daily tasks from the wheelbarrow – a much smaller, more manageable load. Decision-making will be faster. You will feel less overwhelmed.

As you roll your way through the week and get things done, your wheelbarrow will be getting lighter. At the same time, others will also be tossing in new demands. Having already narrowed your focus for the week, you'll find it easier to compare the surprises with the planned tasks and change your plans to handle the new tasks or renegotiate as necessary.

This approach doesn't mean that the semi-load of tasks will disappear. It does mean that you will spend less time looking over your shoulder, worrying about being flattened by your very own Mac truck. And that, in itself, is a relief!

"I don't know the key to success, but the key to failure is trying to please everybody."

Bill Cosby

THE BIG PICTURE

PLANNING PITFALLS

"Why bother planning my day? The real day never turns out anything like the plan, anyway. It's depressing to never even get close to the end of the list!"

Sound familiar? If planning is such an important element of success, why is it so frustrating?

Ask yourself if you are subject to one or more of these pitfalls of planning and experiment with the suggested solutions.

Are you overly optimistic about how quickly you can accomplish a task. Do you underestimate how long it will take, forget to allow for inevitable interruptions, or misjudge the complexity of the job when you commit yourself to project deadlines?

Map out the approach in detail. Ask questions of those who have tackled such jobs in the past. Build time for the unexpected into your initial estimates. Track the time on current jobs and use that information to improve your future estimates.

Do you overlook the amount of time in an average workday that is taken up with tasks that you can't predict or control? Client inquiries, service requests, system problems all fall into this category.

Keep a time log for several days to get a feeling for the proportion of time available for planned work and the amount of time that needs to be kept open for the unexpected. If three-quarters of your day is taken up with unpredictable tasks, you will be continuously frustrated if you plan another half day's work on top of those demands.

Are you so accustomed to the routine of your work that you forget to take into account the amount of time that you typically devote to basic tasks – preparing work schedules, reviewing expense claims, stocking up on supplies. Don't forget to include catching up on office news, and taking coffee and washroom breaks.

Track the amount of time you typically spend on recurring routine tasks for the next couple of months. Build that amount of time into your plans for the months ahead.

Are you part of a working group that is unclear about its purpose or direction, or in which the priorities change by the day or by the hour?

Speak up. Ask questions of clarification. Write your own list of priorities and check it out with others. Develop the habit of asking where the new task fits into the most recent list of priorities. Make it clear that adding higher priorities is going to delay action on other parts of your work.

Do you work with colleagues or supervisors who pass along tasks at random – at all hours of the day – blowing any plans you may have made right out of the water?

Describe the problems created by the ongoing last minute delegation of tasks. Suggest that you meet with key colleagues on a regular basis (at the beginning or end of the day or week). Use that time to check out priorities and delegate work back and forth rather than doing it in such an ad hoc manner.

Are the individual items that show up on your daily plan much larger than anyone could hope to accomplish in the course of one working day? Building a bridge, planning a conference or hiring an assistant are all examples of tasks that fall into this category.

Break it down into smaller more manageable tasks. Hiring an assistant? Write a job description today. Develop an advertisement tomorrow. Place the ad on Friday.

Do you lack enthusiasm for the work in front of you? Has it become routine and boring to the point where distractions are the most welcome part of your day?

Think about what it would take for you to get excited about your work again. Do you want to learn new skills? Are you feeling under appreciated? Would a change in environment or schedule make a difference?

Take action. Try a different approach. Put the power of planning to work for you.

THE BIG PICTURE

MIND MAPPING

Mind mapping (also known as patterning or webbing) is a useful tool for planning what you're going to do, what you're going to say (in a report or presentation), or where you're going to start on any given project. It's a way to break major challenges into more manageable pieces.

Use mind mapping to ready yourself for launching a new promotional campaign, reporting at your next staff meeting, planning a trip, organizing a backlog, building a prototype, learning a new skill, or improving relationships with others.

Grab a paper and pen; or, if you prefer to think big, grab a large sheet of newsprint and colored markers or work on a white board. Mind mapping can be tackled solo or in a group.

Begin by naming your goal and assigning a deadline date for completion. Write this information in the center of your page and enclose it in a circle. Suppose, as an example, your goal is to replace the existing office photocopier by September 30.

The next step is to identify the actions that you need to take to bring that goal to completion. Note each different action area at the end of a spoke radiating from the circled goal. Each time you identify a new major category of tasks, start a new arm or spoke on your map. Don't worry about the order in which the tasks need to be tackled, just jot them down as they come to mind.

In this example, main action areas might include: determining usage requirements, arranging financing, disposing of the old copier, listing desirable features, inviting bids from suppliers, collecting current information on copier options, making a purchase decision, and so on.

After you have mapped out the main tasks, list smaller sub-tasks for each area. For example, "Make purchase decision" has been broken down into five sub-tasks.

You've been specific enough in the listing of your sub-tasks if there are actions at this level of your plan that could be handled in 15 minutes or less (e.g., make a phone call to supplier A, stop by the library to pick up a business magazine, start a list of desirable copier features).

Once you've exhausted your first round of thinking, review the major action areas and number them in the order in which they need to be tackled. In the case of our copier example, the main areas have been numbered from one to eight.

Keeping your final deadline in mind, assign intermediate deadlines to each of the main action areas. If it is now the first week in August and you plan to have the new machine in place by September 30, you might want to complete your preliminary research by August 10 and determine usage and feature requirements by August 15.

The mapping technique meets many of the criteria for effective goal setting. A map is specific and written. It notes deadline dates and breaks the project down into a series of smaller tasks. Seeing the detail involved in any project helps you carry out a reality check. Determine whether the plan is feasible given the other demands on your time – and whether you need to move more quickly or extend your final deadline. By posting your map in a visible spot, you can make certain that it is reviewed as you move forward.

Fleshing out the details of a major project in this way makes delegation and team cooperation on projects easier to manage. All those involved can see how the various parts of the project fit together and understand the potential impact of meeting or missing intermediate deadlines.

PRODUCTIVITY PRINCIPLES

PRIME TIME

Have you ever worked with someone who would arrive at work well before anyone else having already put in three hours at home – mowing the lawn, washing the car and wallpapering the front hall?

Perhaps you've shared an office with someone who was pretty much incoherent until after his second cup of coffee – a person who really hit his stride just as the official work day was winding down for everyone else?

If so, then you've met a couple of real life examples of prime time in action.

Prime time is that period of the day when your energy is high and your mind is clear. During your prime time, you are at your freshest. You are most capable of working through complicated problems and tough issues.

Most people can readily identify their period of prime time as occurring in one of these slots: early or mid morning, afternoon, evening or late at night.

If you aren't sure what part of the day constitutes your prime time, pay close attention to your levels of concentration for several days. Every waking hour, on the hour, rate your ability to focus on a scale of 1 to 10 where 1 is "Getting nowhere fast!" and 10 means "Hang on to your hats – I'm coming through!"

To increase your effectiveness and productivity, you want to make the best possible use of your prime time. Commit as much of that time as possible to projects that are high priority items. Use it to move forward on projects that aren't yet urgent but could be very important to your satisfaction or success.

At the very least, don't give your prime time away. Avoid using it to sort paperwork, sift through memos, or catch up on general reading. Don't spend prime time on lengthy coffee breaks or the social chitchat that is a part of daily office life.

Don't commit yourself to attending meetings during that part of the day, with people who have a reputation for going on far too long with far too few results.

If you are a prime time morning person and a colleague with a poor track record for meeting effectiveness calls to arrange a get-together for 9:30 tomorrow morning, defend your prime time.

Tell the caller that 2:00 in the afternoon would be better for you. Don't be shy about making the request. Most people are quite flexible, because most people have no plan at all.

Share prime time information with colleagues. Perhaps you can work out a trade. Once a week a colleague spends an hour during your prime time covering your phone calls, drop-in visitors and other unexpected interruptions.

You are free to disappear behind a closed door or head down the hall to work in an empty conference room for a gloriously uninterrupted sixty minutes.

Once a week you return the favor. Both parties benefit from increased productivity and reduced frustration.

"We all have times when we think more effectively, and times when we should not be thinking at all."

Daniel Cohen

PRODUCTIVITY PRINCIPLES

BUNCHING

Valuable hours are lost every day in wasted "set up" and "take down" time.

Each time you get ready to do a task, you gear up for it – mentally and physically. You re-orient your thoughts as you put away the materials from the last task and pull out the materials you need for the next job. You physically make the switch in work location and body position.

The grasshopper approach – hopping back and forth between tasks – can be costly. Think "bunches and groups" instead of jumping randomly from one thing to another.

The practice of bunching or grouping is to time management what compound interest is to financial planning – a magic multiplier. Here's how it works.

You're checking through your paperwork and come across a question you need to check with a colleague. It's not urgent, but you call immediately and get the answer to your question.

Ten minutes later another question surfaces and you call the same person again. Fifteen minutes later you repeat the process for a third time.

In less than half an hour, you've now interrupted the same colleague three times. By applying the bunching principle, you could have accumulated questions for that individual throughout the morning and handled all three questions with one call.

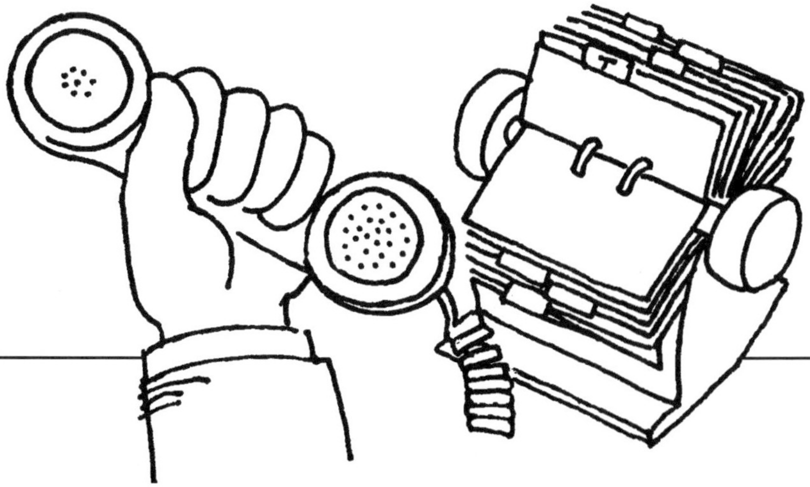

Suppose you have several phone calls to make. You clear a spot on your desk, grab the directory, pull the phone toward you and make the first call.

As you speak, a piece of correspondence catches your eye. When you finish the first call, you push the phone to the back corner of your desk. You pick up the stray paper, read it, make a few notes, pull out some background information and set the bundle of papers aside.

Then you clear a spot on the desk, grab the phone directory, pull down the phone, and move on to call number two.

To bunch, place as many calls as possible at the same time. When you do this, your mind is already in telephone mode and you've got your directory, phone, rolodex and note paper at hand.

When you're dealing with the finances, you could choose to pay each bill on the day it comes in – getting out the chequebook, finding an envelope and stamp, putting it all away again every time there's an invoice in the mail. Or you could save up all the bills and sit down to pay them once a week – cutting back considerably on the set up and take down time.

To apply the grouping principle to other office paperwork, collect non-urgent materials to be photocopied or faxed and make a single run before lunch and a second run at the end of the day.

Bunch correspondence and dictate all replies at one sitting.

Collect all materials that require a quick review and signature in a "To Sign" folder and handle them at set intervals through the day.

Bunching is effective outside the office as well. Suppose it's Saturday. A quick trip to the office, yard work, lawn mowing and socializing are on your agenda for the day.

You work in the yard for an hour or two; and then you change into something more presentable to drop in at the office. Arriving home, you change back into yard clothes to mow the lawn. An hour later, you're changing yet again to go out for coffee.

To apply the bunching principle, you would reorder the day's activities to minimize the number of wardrobe changes. For example, you might do all the yard work first and stop at the office later when you head out for coffee.

PRODUCTIVITY PRINCIPLES

Expansion Joints

Expansion joints smooth the lumps and bumps on the roads we travel every day.

Felted fibers are cast between slabs of concrete in driveways and sidewalks. Mesh fingers and overlapping steel strips connect sections of bridges.

Why are they there? Because not everything in this world shifts and changes at the same rate.

Expansion joints would be quite unnecessary if steel and concrete were to expand and shrink at the same rate under the same conditions. But that's not the way the world works.

As individuals, we don't always respond in the same way to the same conditions or to conditions that change from day to day or hour by hour.

Adding expansion joints to our daily plans can keep us from buckling under the stress and pressure.

Although the standard commute to work may take 10 minutes, if you allow 15 minutes you'll build in a buffer that lets you take poor road conditions, stalled cars and slow moving trains in stride.

When setting a time to leave the house, allow five extra minutes to account for the "lost sneaker factor". There will usually be something that delays you on your way out the door (a last-minute phone call, missing keys, forgotten paperwork or runaway sneakers).

When you include small children in your plans, you can be sure that the wee ones will need a bathroom at the very moment that the facilities are farthest away. The same youngsters that will cruise at full speed all day on the playground will quickly become tired and cranky when trailing behind you on adult errands. Factor in enough buffer time to allow for extra breaks.

For sizable undertakings and for projects where a large number of variables are beyond your control, you want to build in king-size expansion joints.

When planning major events, add an extra 20% to your time estimates, so you have room to maneuver when the pressure is on.

When scheduling coffee and lunch breaks for a sizable conference program, add an extra five minutes to the coffee breaks and an extra fifteen minutes to the lunch break. When program expansion joints are too small, you end up with frustrated participants and an agenda that runs late.

When delegating parts of a project, build in buffer zones at various stages along the way, so that a delay on the part of one individual will not throw the entire plan out of whack.

When using public transportation, make scheduling choices to avoid those fast dashes between commitments.

Don't book yourself on a flight that leaves 45 minutes after your meeting is due to end, when you know the meeting room is 30 minutes from the airport. Meetings run long and airplanes don't always run late.

Reward yourself when an expansion joint does its job. On those occasions when you arrive somewhere with a few minutes to spare, make a phone call to a friend, spend a few minutes with a book, or simply relax and watch the rest of the world rushing to catch up.

There are very fine lines between wasting time, scheduling for efficiency, and living on the run. Expansion joints help optimize that balance.

"Nothing can be more useful to a man than a determination not to be hurried."

Henry David Thoreau

PRODUCTIVITY PRINCIPLES

Custom Repeats

Every office has them. Those tedious tasks that come around again and again. Forward planning makes those "Oh, no! Not this again!" jobs easier to bear.

If you file annual claims or reports, take a moment to flag invoices and documents that will be needed later. Index them with post-it notes as they are filed or shunt them into a special holding folder.

When you track participation or response statistics, note the numbers as you conduct or wind up the programs, activities or promotions. The information will still be fresh and close at hand.

As you orient someone to new responsibilities, alert that person to information that should be recorded through the year. It's better to know what's needed sooner than later. If you are taking on a new position, ask your predecessor what needs to be tracked and how that information is used.

Check out your record-keeping habits to see where you might streamline your operation. Are you recording the same name, address and phone information in several different software programs (a contact manager, an invoicing program, a fax directory)? Can you find ways to integrate the systems so the information need only be entered once and transferred automatically?

If you need to collect specific data (on the origin of calls or types of inquiries, for example), set up and distribute a checksheet ahead of time so everyone is working with the same format. Compiling the results will take less time.

Design short forms or form letters to handle repeat requests for information and messages that are sent frequently.

A pre-inked stamp can be a time-saver. Order one with your name, company, address and phone number. Use it to complete warranties, product registration cards and subscription forms.

Remember to revise the information that appears on your business forms each time they are reprinted. Do you need to add tax or fax numbers or an on-line address to your new business stationary?

Customize your keyboard. If there are phrases or paragraphs that you use repeatedly, set word processing commands so you are able to pop those units into your documents with a single keystroke.

If you repeatedly send cheques to the same suppliers, or invoices to the same clients, be sure that their names and addresses can be called up instantly on your system. Preprint reasonable quantities of mailing labels for each office or individual with whom you communicate often.

Be on the look-out for merry-go-round activities. Each time you come face to face with one of those recurring tasks, stop and ask yourself how you could cut down on the time it takes to handle this job. It all adds up!

"We are what we repeatedly do."
Aristotle

PRODUCTIVITY PRINCIPLES

FORWARD MOTION

The old Ed Sullivan Show showcased comedians, music and novelty acts. One novelty act that appeared with some regularity was the plate spinner.

This fellow would pick up one dinner plate after another and set each one spinning at the end of its own long stick. He then attempted to keep them all in motion at once, racing from stick to stick accompanied by appropriately dramatic music and a chorus of oohs and aahs.

Few of us are backed up by a ten-piece orchestra, but the challenge of daily life and work is much the same for us as it was for the aspiring plate spinner. The difference is that we would rather not be racing around in circles – as entertaining as that might be to others.

Billie Jean King, famed tennis player, cautioned that one should "never confuse movement with action". The difference, it would seem, involves a question of direction and purpose. Does the motion move things forward?

This principle of forward motion is a useful one in getting things done. It keeps projects from stalling out or grinding to a halt. It prevents work and living spaces from being smothered by the stuff of life.

Forward motion involves identifying and taking "the next step".

A letter sits on the corner of your desk awaiting your reply. You need more information before you can put together your answer. If you were to apply the principle of forward motion, you could place a call to the library reference department, check your own reference books, or ask someone else to scout out the information you need.

A colleague wants to meet with you to discuss a joint project. Your time is booked solidly this week, so you've put off making a commitment. Setting a specific meeting time and agenda for next week would move things forward.

You are headed for the files to retrieve a contract. As you pass the "To Be Filed" basket, you notice a report that belongs in the same file. You grab the report from the basket, take it with you, and pop it in the file as you retrieve the contract.

The hammer you used to hang a picture in the office is still sitting on the top of your bookcase. It belongs in the workshop at home. You are not on your way home, however you are cutting through the parking lot on your way to a business meeting. Take the hammer and drop it in the car so it's one step closer to its destination.

For some time, you've been wanting to pull together a procedures manual that would be helpful for beginning staff. Time is short and it seems like a big project. Instead of doing nothing, start jotting down the steps involved in various procedures as you carry them out in your daily work. Encourage co-workers to do the same. Collect the individual pages of notes in one file and watch the procedures guide write itself over the next six months.

The principle of forward motion is a bit like hitchhiking. It revolves around small actions in the right direction – one step at a time.

"The business of life is to go forward."

Samuel Johnson

ACTION TOOLS

PICKING A PLANNER

What started out as a simple listing of 365 days divided into 12 months has evolved into a mini industry. The range of choice for tools to use in tracking the details of your life is mind boggling.

The first decision is a basic one. Are you looking for a calendar that provides day, date, month and a space to note the event of the day? Or do you need a planner to coordinate the details of your life?

Simple calendars can be found everywhere. Finding the right planner is more of a challenge.

Inventory your needs and preferences before you go hunting or you're sure to return muddleheaded and emptyhanded. Choose a personal planning calendar that complements the way you work and think.

If your day planner will travel with you, it needs to be portable enough to tuck into your briefcase, pocket or purse.

Pick a format that supports your most important functions. Do you schedule many daily appointments? Do you track billing time? Do you block out time to work on projects? Do you use your calendar pages as a reminder for follow-ups?

At a minimum, planners should provide enough space to record each day's appointments, phone calls, errands and priority tasks. Will straight calendar pages suffice? How much extra information do you need to have at hand? Do you need access to telephone numbers, expense records or goals?

Loose-leaf binders make it easy to move material in and out if you need that kind of flexibility.

You and your planner will be seeing a lot of each other. Pick a style you like to look at and use – whether it's serious and professional or a more lighthearted format.

Planning systems range in price from the $1.49 "Year At a Glance" unit to the $300.00 "This Is Your Life" model. Weigh the cost against the potential return and remember this will be an annual expense.

Choose the minimum system that does the job. If extra options don't work for you, they're dead weight and don't belong in your planner.

If you can't find a commercial version that fits your workstyle, design your own calendar pages. Consider using some of these headings: Do, Call, See, Write, Appointments, Personal, Expenses, Errands and Notes.

Customize your own planning system for the price of a binder (they come in all sizes), a loose-leaf refill, a set of indexed dividers and copies of your own calendar pages. Label the sections according to your own needs: Daily Calendar/To Do, Goals, Errands & Odd Jobs, Major Projects, Shopping, Books, Gift Ideas, Correspondence, etc.

Add a file or zip-lock pocket to hold a pen, expense receipts and pickup stubs.

There are several digital diaries on the market. These pocket-sized electronic organizers, complete with alarms, provide a record of daily activities and commitments. They house a card file of business contacts and offer memo space for reminders and lists. Some digital diaries interface with desktop computers and printers for updating a computerized office calendar and printing a record of the day's schedule.

Whatever your choice, work from only one personal calendar. Too many calendars mean too much confusion.

"Being organized is not an end in itself – it is a vehicle to take you from where you are to where you want to be."

Stephanie Winston

ACTION TOOLS

THE ELECTRONIC ASSISTANT

The P.C. (Personal Computer) is everywhere. Whether you refer to your P.C. as "My Buddy, Max" or "Throckmorton, My Faithful Butler", today's computer is every business person's good right hand.

Computer use in the business world is so widespread and common place that a computer is just as much of a basic business tool as the telephone and filing cabinet. These suggestions will help you make the most of your electronic assistant.

Your choice of computer and software depends on the kinds of work you perform. Before choosing a machine, take stock of your needs.

Do you want your assistant to be able to take care of: word processing, data and file management, accounting or bookkeeping, scheduling and planning, communications, research, publishing, or making presentations?

Sort the various functions into "must have" and "would be nice" categories. Zero in on the most important ones. Look for software programs that will meet those highest priority needs.

Once you've narrowed your choice of software, you will have already started to narrow the choices in the hardware field.

Before making your final decision, consider: cost, warranty and service, dealer and manufacturer reputation, and the amount of time that will be required to learn to use the system.

Think about mobility, too. If your work involves traveling, and you plan to manage your projects or appointment schedule on the computer, you may want to consider a laptop – or a smaller companion electronic organizer that can be linked to communicate with your desktop computer.

Once you and your computer have been formally introduced, invest a few hours in learning how your assistant thinks and works.

Read the manuals that accompany your most critical programs. Ask experienced users about their shortcuts. Be on the look out for customizing possibilities.

Find your own computer mentor and guide – someone who is familiar with your type of system, knowledgeable about the programs, and not so carried away with the magic of computing that their answers are unintelligible to the average slo-tech mortal.

Keep yourself informed about "add-on" options. A scanner (especially one that comes with optical character recognition) might be helpful in managing reference information. A separate label printer could help with your mailing and filing.

Recognize that upgrade mania is a driving force in the world of computing. Before you put your money down for any new improved versions, be clear about the benefits that you expect to receive from the upgrades.

Will the new equipment or software significantly improve the quality of your work, save time and energy, or make a sizable difference in your client service abilities?

What is the purchase dollar cost? What other costs are involved in changing and learning about the new system?

Remember that all upgrades, even to software with which you are already familiar, will take time to learn if you want to get the expected benefits. Plan appropriately.

Check for hidden spin-off costs associated with the upgrade. Perhaps the "new improved" word processing package is so large that it will slow your system and require an extra hardware investment.

This information is available from sales reps., fellow computer users, and the manufacturers themselves. Ask questions. It will save you time and money.

ACTION TOOLS

POST IT

The term, "post it", used to mean "find a mail box and drop it in the slot". Now it means, write a reminder on a small slip of paper and find someplace to stick it.

Those little yellow Post-It devils have taken over the world. You'll find office desks, computer terminals, cash registers, bulletin boards, and kitchen refrigerators all papered with sticky note reminders.

What started out as a good idea for temporary messages has ended up creating a permanent clutter of its own.

In fact, it's hard to remember "life before Post-Its"; and the little yellow stickies have grown to meet the demands.

Post-It notes are now available in a variety of sizes (as small as 1" x 2" and as large as 4" x 6"). The larger size is good news for folks who find a short note turning into a long chain of teeny Post-Its.

Colors range from pale pastels to neon brights. Post-It notes will lie quietly on your desk or pop vigorously from dispensers. You'll find Post-Its printed with advertising reminders, funny sayings and decorative illustrations.

The sticky strip has been added to many preprinted office forms: phone message pads, routing slips, filing instructions, and fax labels. Even desktop and drawer organizers have been redesigned to accommodate the little stickers.

There's no doubt that Post-Its are convenient. You no longer need to search for tape or a tack to post a message; and

there is little danger of loose messages being blown away by sudden gusts of wind.

But if you stop and think about this for a moment, just how many messages need to be hung in the first place? And how many people work in offices where gusts of wind are even remotely likely?

This fascination with the convenient Post-It can be expensive. A Post-It phone message slip can cost ten times as much as the non-stick variety.

Cost aside, there are situations in which these little wonders are worth their weight in gold.

Post brief notes as short-term reminders of tasks in a compact calendar or date book.

Use Post-Its as flags to mark important information in books, magazines and reports.

Use them to customize seminar presentations by posting examples appropriate for your current audience next to the point being illustrated.

Write ideas on index-card-sized sticky notes (one idea per note) when brainstorming with a group. Post the ideas on a nearby wall for review. They are easily rearranged and regrouped by priority, activity, cost or time.

Keep a pad in the car to jot down route directions and addresses, list errands and leave notes on people's front doors. (It could also be handy for commenting on the skill of the driver parked next to you in a crowded parkade.)

Add post-its to the medicine cabinet to use when leaving notes on the bathroom mirror for other family members. This one suggestion alone could raise the art of "nagging by note" to a whole new level. Washroom Post-Its could also be used to note supplies that should be added to the shopping list and to record ideas that bubble to the surface while soaking in the tub.

Stick a Post-It pad in the drawer of the front hall table to jot reminders of errands and items to take with you on your way out the door.

Since a Post-It is useless without a pen or pencil, you may want to tether a pencil to each pad.

If you like the convenience of the Post-It note, but are concerned about the price, follow the lead of a resourceful acquaintance who writes each note at the bottom of the larger Post-Its so she can tear off the first message and recycle the note for one or two more uses. Now that's economy!

ACTION TOOLS

STOCKING UP

The arrival of a new office supply catalogue or the occasional tour of a stationary store always generates a few new time, effort and dollar-saving possibilities. Be sure to check out the new product lines once or twice a year.

Color-coded index sets for 3-ring binders are an excellent innovation. Each divider is color tabbed, and a corresponding color-coded index page is provided with each set. Simply photocopy a master table of contents onto the colored index page. Presto, an instant reference to the various sections of the binder without having to type and stuff tiny cardboard tags into tiny vinyl tabs.

Every fax message does not need a full-page letter of introduction. Lay out your letters and memos to accommodate Post-It Fax Notes. Stick one on the corner of the first page to summarize the transmission details.

If you're having trouble spotting the labels on your hanging file folders, it could be that the folders sitting inside the hanging "hammocks" are riding too high.

Invest in a box or two of specially designed interior file folders. They're slightly shorter than regulation-size folders. Because they sit a half-inch below the tabs, flush with the top line of the hanging folders, they won't interfere with your view of the labels.

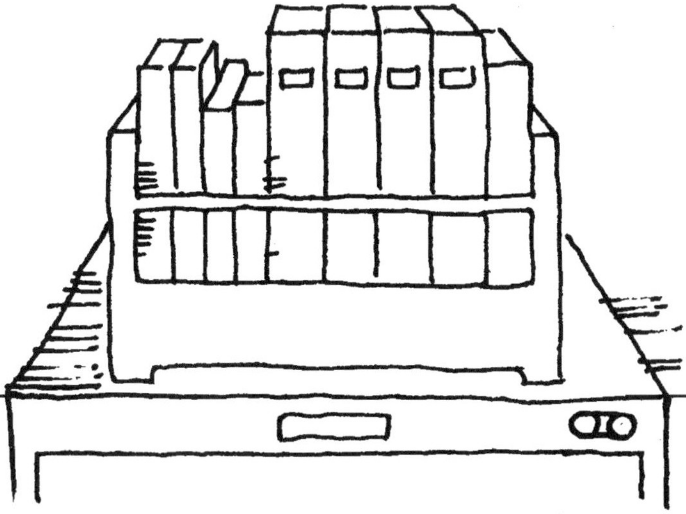

If you use a lot of overhead transparencies in your presentations, Flip Frames are a great alternative to the cardboard mounts that are typically used to frame overhead transparencies.

A Flip Frame is an acetate pocket into which you slip your transparency. Opaque white "wings" flip out on both sides to block the projector light around the sides of the transparency and frame the image in the center.

The frames are three-hole punched and much more compact than the bulky cardboard mounts. They are easily filed in a three-ring binder for storage on a standard bookshelf.

Planning sessions really chew up the newsprint flipchart. If you're concerned about conservation, try the vinyl flipchart that works like an erasable whiteboard. Just wipe away your plans with a whiteboard brush or cloth. The statically charged vinyl sheets will stick to smooth walls without tape.

Tired of trying to keep that collection of binders, directories and supply catalogues from sliding off the top of your filing cabinets? Pick up a set of metal book ends with a built in magnetic base. Once you set them down on top of a metal file cabinet, they won't be going anywhere fast.

If you are looking for an alternative to paper clipping or stapling business cards to small quantities of brochures, flyers and presentation folders, check out the punch that slices two diagonal slots on regular paper or heavier cover stock. Just slide your business card into the slots and fire the item off to your client.

Does your phone book keep falling off the shelf or sliding across your desk? Look for a clear acrylic stand that holds a desktop phone on its slanted top and houses the phone book underneath the platform. No need to be digging the phone book out of the side drawer or trying to train the floppy pages to stand upright on a bookshelf; and the tilted top makes it easier to use the keypad on the phone.

Tired of carrying dog-eared photos or business cards in your wallet or deciphering recipe cards smeared with ingredients from the past? Check out a desktop pouch laminator that handles items up to four inches in width (from business and credit cards to photos and recipes). Use it to make your own durable luggage tags – for business travel or client gifts.

"Chaos is optional."

Jann Mitchell

OFFICE ORGANIZATION

OFFICE CENTERS

Shopping centers! Rec centers! Seniors' centers! What's in a center? It could be almost anything.

The important point is that each center provides a focus for a certain kind of activity. The center concept is an important one in office organization.

If you feel as if you're constantly searching for the right tool or performing one task on top of another, it may be time to center yourself and your space.

Begin by listing the key functions performed in the office. Do you keep the books, handle mail or package goods, track inventory, file resource information, or spend time planning and meeting with others?

Group working materials and equipment around your most critical centers of operation.

A communications center could revolve around your phone, answering machine and fax. It might include your rolodex, phone book, postal code directory, fax routing notes, dictation equipment, and phone message pads.

A mail-handling center could include: a letter opener, packing envelopes, labels, filament tape, scissors, string, date stamp, postal scale and meter, and baskets for mail in transit.

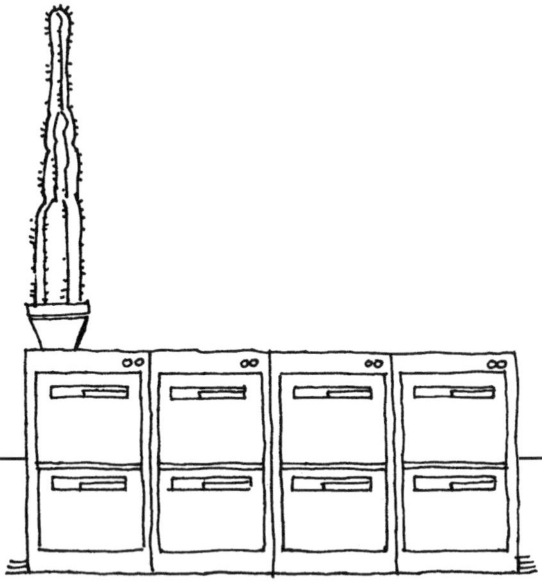

A computer center could include cleaning supplies for diskettes, keyboard and disk drive as well as software reference books.

A printing and copying center could be set up around the copier and computer printer. It may include: copy paper, letterhead, friction feed forms, scrap paper bins, toner and glass cleaner.

A finance center would serve as the collection point for bills and receipts. Checkbooks, deposit slips, cash box, ledgers, account statements and printouts would all be grouped in the vicinity.

A meeting or planning center might include a white board, flip chart, a large wall calendar, a meeting table and chairs.

A reference center would house books, magazines and journals, video and audio tapes, and reference files.

A supply and storage center would accommodate extra stationary materials, and back-up office and cleaning supplies.

Just like NASA, every office needs a launch center. This could be an open shelf or tabletop that provides a temporary resting place for your briefcase and traveling supplies, materials you are collecting for an upcoming project, handouts that are duplicated and ready to go to an upcoming meeting, or files waiting to be returned to a colleague.

Some of these centers develop naturally as responsibilities are divided and delegated. Others need to be deliberately masterminded.

Several centers may share the same space. For example, the communications and computer areas may be combined if you operate a fax modem or maintain client names and contact information on your computer.

Other centers may best be located next to or across from each other. A mail-handling center and an order-filling center may share a common pool of wrapping materials, labels and packaging supplies.

As you consider the placement of various work centers, take a second look at your furnishings. Trading in a tall four drawer file cabinet for two shorter cabinets will create an extra working surface at desk height.

Consider grouping desks and tables in L-shapes or U-shapes to bring frequently used centers within arm's reach.

"If you don't know you have it, or

can't find it, it is of no value to you."

Hemphill's Principle

OFFICE ORGANIZATION

DESKTOP DISORDER

What image does your desktop bring to mind?

A lot of desktops look like the rugged Rocky Mountains – with very high peaks and very deep valleys. Large-scale avalanches are just a bump away.

Other desktops are reminiscent of birds' nests or foxholes. One small open space is banked by papers, books, coffee cups, souvenirs, snacks, photos, small office appliances and miscellaneous doodads.

If you find that you need a map to navigate the top of your desk, or that co-workers are hanging messages from helium balloons to catch your attention, it could be time for a tune-up.

Start by making a clean sweep of the desk area. Remove everything from your desktop and look closely at the collection.

Select the items you use constantly. Set them on the most accessible areas of your desk. If you use your calculator every 10 minutes, it deserves prime space (on the right side if you are right handed). If you only use a calculator once every 10 days, it belongs somewhere else.

Store those infrequently used items out of sight (in desk drawers or on neighboring shelves). An object has to be important and earn its keep to occupy prime desktop space.

If your desk is up against the wall, place a short, shallow hutch on the back of your desktop. Tuck small equipment and supplies (calculator, rolodex, note pads) in the space created. Keep your lamp, phone, date book and coffee cup on top.

Don't clutter up your desktop with duplicate supplies. Follow the "One In Service" principle. Keep on top just one each of the common office items that you use.

The well-stocked office desk contains the items you use – not a representative stationary store sample of goods. If you don't use highlighters, don't keep them at your desk.

Dump those bulky boxes that house master copies of software long since installed on the hard drive. Shelve the current manuals, store the master disks, and junk the handbooks for outdated versions of your software.

If you work back and forth between a number of different projects at the same time, house each project in its own banker's box or purchase desktop standing file holders to keep each set of materials separate but close at hand.

When you work on a major project over a long period of time, you may wish to devote a separate work area or side table to that one task. You can leave those materials open and ready for action without having to move them to the side while you deal with everyday business on your main desk.

Pay attention to disorderly piles that accumulate on ledges and tabletops. Set up trays to accommodate the varied categories of materials: papers that are being rerouted home, files that have been purged in the daily course of business and are waiting for a trip to the archives.

Designate a permanent and prominent location for your planning notebook or "things to do" list. If you slip it into the bottom drawer of your desk for safe-keeping, it won't help keep you on track through the day.

Use desk drawer space effectively. Install a stationary holder to separate the papers and forms used frequently. Set a "catch-all" organizer tray in a desk drawer to hold small items that are used infrequently.

Treat yourself to one desk top item that's good for the soul – an interesting plant, your "hole-in-one" golf ball, a photo of your favorite place or person. It's an excellent daily reminder, as you keep your nose to the grindstone, that there is much more to life than work, alone!

OFFICE ORGANIZATION

"In" Basket Insights

Contrary to common usage, "In" does not mean indefinite, insufferable, or infinite. Nor does it stand for insomnia – although there are those folks who do lose sleep over their "In" baskets.

An alarming number of office '"In" baskets are managed by graduates of the Composting School of Paper Flow.

The CSP approach to paperhandling works like this. Pile it up. Aerate daily. When the stack is well aged, spread it around. Cross your fingers and hope that good things grow.

The original "In" basket was designed to be a place for others to deposit incoming messages and papers. Think of the "In" basket as a desktop mail box – a place from which to retrieve the daily news – not a long-term storage unit.

Indecision is the main cause of "In" basket overflow. Papers are repeatedly tossed back into the bin because the receiver isn't sure what to do with them.

The keys to dealing successfully with the daily influx of paper are to be more decisive and to set up a system based on progressive action.

Place five other bins in the vicinity of your desk: a large garbage basket, a recycling bin for waste paper, a "Read" basket

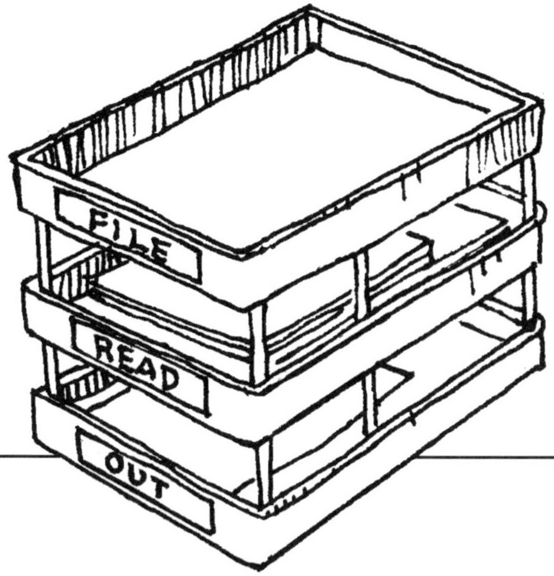

in which you'll toss general reading materials that have no deadlines attached, an "Out" basket for papers to be rerouted to others, and a "File" basket for inactive papers and reference materials that will eventually be filed away.

Daily sorting of incoming papers using those basic five containers will likely cut the contents of your "In" basket in half.

For the remaining materials, ask yourself this question: "What is the next action that is needed on this piece of paper?"

Typical answers include these types of actions: hold until Jim calls back, discuss at staff meeting, take to the photocopier, send by fax, approve for payment, add signature, write a letter, place a call.

Create a set of action file folders labeled with your most common next steps: Calls to Make, Waiting For Callback, Correspondence To Dictate, To Sign, To Copy, To Fax, Staff Meeting, Payables. "Upcoming Events" is useful for temporarily holding meeting notices, program schedules and tickets.

Create folders with the names of your supervisor, employees, key colleagues and any other individuals with whom you are in regular contact.

Set up a folder for each new project so you have a designated spot in which to deposit working materials and new information related to that activity.

Keep these action files in the open side drawer of your desk, a freestanding desktop unit, or a vertical file holder that sits on a return or the corner of your desk. Action files need to be within arm's reach so that you can be in and out of them through the work day.

Each day as you work your way through the newly arrived materials in your "In" basket, either handle them immediately or deposit them in the appropriate folders for future action. If you are worried that you may forget about an item because the paper is out of sight, use your planning notebook or calendar to note reminders of tasks yet to be done.

Individuals who handle date-specific papers may wish to set up a set of tickler files – one for each day of the month (1-31). File items by the dates on which they need to be handled and check the tickler file each morning.

A good set of action and tickler files clears out the "In" basket and reduces tedious searching and sifting. When you are ready to place calls, the messages are all in one place. When Jim returns your call, the paper you want to discuss with him can easily be pulled from the Waiting-For-Callback file.

OFFICE ORGANIZATION

THE ALL OUT OPTION

If the very thought of a sterile, barren desktop makes you break into a cold sweat, relax.

As you may or may not have noticed from your vantage point in the trenches, the "clear the decks and file it away" approach to office organization is not for everyone.

Some perfectly capable and very creative individuals have never filed a piece of paper in their lives. They operate visually associating information with colors, textures, timing and positions.

"Those papers by the phone are waiting for phone calls. That stack on the left-hand corner of the desk is about a business trip being planned to the southwest."

"Oh, there's the red file on the Smith project. I must think of a couple of ideas to suggest at next week's meeting. The Wilson Report? Let's see, it arrived about the same time as the last industry newsletter, so it's going to be right over here."

These "everything-out" folks are often very good at retrieving information. The visual reminders keep projects percolating in the recesses of their minds – generating ideas as they mentally skip between projects.

While the self-induced interruptions of an "all-over-the place" office might drive "one-thing-at-a-time" folks bonkers, the system works just fine for many. The most difficult hurdle in this style of operation is generating enough tabletop holding space.

There are organizing tools that will free up horizontal working space and let you keep tabs on the whereabouts of projects without having to file them out of sight.

Multi-compartment desktop hutches are one option. Nine-compartment cardboard shoe organizers that can be found in the housewares section of department stores will also work well. Make certain that they're large enough to accommodate the width of a standard paper or file folder.

Literature sorters (the kind designed for holding product spec sheets, brochures, and flyers) can be set at the back of a table or desk and used to hold papers and projects without having to hide them away.

Invest in clear Lucite boxes or containers. Consider mounting a couple of transparent "hot files" (slanted holding bins) on the wall beside your desk. Use them to group certain kinds of business-in-progress that you don't want to forget. Some hot files are equipped with magnets for easy attachment to the sides of metal filing cabinets.

If you are in frequent danger of misplacing your reminders of things to be done today, try using an upright stand that can't be buried under the sea of paper. Clip your list to it or group your post-it reminders in categories on the face of the stand.

In team-oriented work places, work often moves back and forth between colleagues. If you and your co-workers have wildly different styles of desk and office management, you need to talk.

Give your co-workers a tour of your desktop and your system – especially if it's one of those "no-obvious-system" systems. Let them know how your work is arranged.

If you don't like people messing with your style of organization, or it bothers you that co-workers dump messages and papers in the middle of your work area every time you step out for a moment, speak up. Suggest other options.

Some folks place an "In-Basket Mail Box" by their door so that others can drop off items for their attention without interfering with "work in progress".

If you subscribe to the "spread-the-work-around-and-pile-it-up" method of desktop organization, be aware of the impact of your organizational style on others.

Don't use your preference for visible stacks and piles as an excuse for hanging on to materials that have long since outlived their usefulness. Pay attention to how long it takes to retrieve information. When those retrieval times start eating into your productivity, it's definitely time to regroup, sort and clear stuff out.

OFFICE ORGANIZATION

SHARED WORK SPACES

In the days of large families, sharing a bedroom with a sibling or two was common practice. It provided a hands-on introduction to the intricacies of setting boundaries, protecting territory and settling border disputes.

Now that families are smaller, sharing bedrooms is less of an issue. However, sharing space at work is becoming more and more common. Job sharing, cross-training and the trend to part-time or contract work all mean that co-workers often share the same office, desk, or work station.

The guerrilla tactics of our youth are not exactly appropriate in the work place. Short of laying a line of tape down the middle of the desk, how do you successfully share space with co-workers?

Sometimes, work place policy and design set the standard. Retail check-outs and bank work stations are examples of this approach. Employees adapt to a fixed layout and design, and are able to move in and out of identical stations with ease.

When you share a work space and its layout and organization is within your control, the working arrangements are not quite so straight forward. You'll need to swap preferences and negotiate.

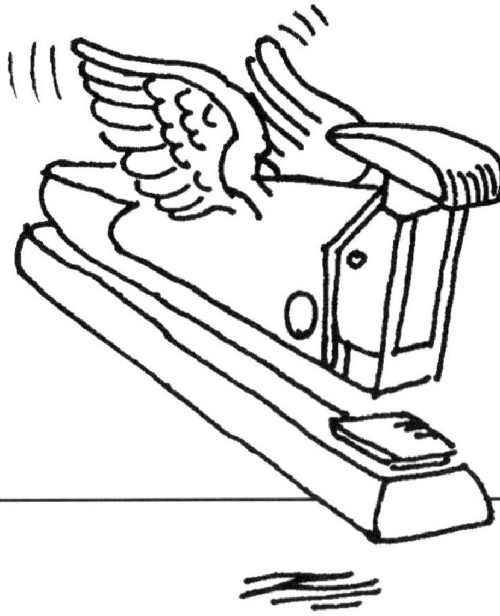

You like flowers. Your office mate is allergic to pollen. You trade in the fresh-cut posies for silk plants.

You are left handed and your work space partner is right handed. When the placement of the phone and the calculator is convenient for you, it will be awkward for your partner. You may agree to simply move the equipment back and forth, setting up for your replacement as you leave for the day. Or you may work from opposite sides of the same table with the equipment in the center – perfectly positioned for both of you.

Your co-worker likes to see everything at once and spreads papers all over the office. You prefer a tidy environment and like to focus on one project at a time. You'll both need to learn to tolerate a different style – especially if you are work in the same spot during the same hours. A visual division of the space (portable dividers, tall filing cabinets, re-orientation of desks) may help reduce conflicts.

If you are using the same space at different times, you may want to divvy up the storage: two desk drawers and shelves for you and two for your partner.

Travelling office supplies are a common frustration. You always leave the stapler in the same spot in the desk drawer, while your partner believes in creative deposition (dropping items wherever they were last used).

If space and budget allow, try the travelling cash drawer approach. Each of you maintains your own drawer, box or tray of small office supplies (stapler, sticky notes, pens, scissors). It travels with you and is hands off to your partner.

Short on work space? Take a close look at your furnishings. Trade a standard desk (that only accommodates one person at a time) for a wider table at which two people can work across from each other.

Occasionally, you may want to scout out a less crowded or quieter spot in which to work. An empty boardroom or a spare utility table could fit the bill. A cordless phone, a desktop file unit or a three-tiered supply basket on wheels will make your work more portable.

Keep in mind that there is more than one "right" way to organize a work space. Tolerance for differences is important. So is communication. When something bothers you, speak up and look for a solution that suits both of you.

"Everybody is somebody's difficult person."

Rick Brinkman

THE PRINTED WORD

CORRESPONDENCE...DESPONDENCE

Are you feeling guilty about those unanswered letters? Does your Reply Pending file now occupy half a file drawer? Clean up on your correspondence with these suggestions.

If you don't need a written record and you do need a quick reply, use the telephone instead.

Electronic mail is great for short-lived notices and memos. There's no paper to clutter up the desk and the note is easily discarded.

Invest in timesaver stationery for business and personal use. Print your business name and address on 5 x 8" notepaper or on multi-part speed letters and memos. Use it for informal handwritten notes. Clip one to material you send out in response to a request for information.

Print personalized postcards with your name and address and your "mug shot" on the message side. Add stamps and carry the cards with you for instant messages, follow ups, and thank you's.

Attach your own preprinted address labels to reply cards and other forms that ask for this basic information. Use a pre-inked "Kwik Stamp" for the same purpose.

Design a check-off note to attach to material you pass on to colleagues. Start with "To, From and Date" at the top and list instructions that you use often: Read and Toss, File, Please Handle, For Follow Up, Return With Comments, FYI, Ouch, Chuckle of the Day, etc.

Set up a Typing Request Form to note all the information that a secretary will need to do the job. List the following: Your Name (if the typing work is pooled); Date In; Date Required (A.S.A.P. not allowed! Give a real date.); Number of copies; Special Instructions (colored paper, special letterhead, enclosures).

Once every three months or so, hit the card shops. When you find a Get Well, Thank You or Sympathy card that you like, buy several. Pick up suitable greeting cards by the box. Set up a tickler file with pocket dividers for each month. Stash the birthday, anniversary and special occasion cards under the appropriate month so you can find them when you need them.

Maintain a "Save-It/Send-It" file. Clip cartoons and newspaper articles. Tuck a little something extra in with your correspondence.

Reply promptly. Set a goal for turn around time on correspondence. Designate a particular time of the day or the week to deal with it.

Handwrite in-house memos. Remember that they don't need to be letter perfect.

Date letters as they come in. You might be surprised to find that a letter that seems like it just arrived has actually been on your desk for two weeks.

Learn to use dictation equipment. Practice using the recorder so that you become comfortable with it. Jot your main points on paper before you begin talking.

Think of your dictation as a first draft. With word processing capabilities, corrections and changes are easy to make. Ask the person who transcribes your tapes for suggestions on improving your dictation style.

Sometimes you may want to forget about transcription and just send the tape itself. Audio messages invite more color and detail.

Take advantage of word-processing options. Design form letters for routine responses. The computer can quickly personalize them. Design templates or style sheets for forms and reports that are used repeatedly.

"Paper is cheap. Reading-and-writing time are expensive."

Dianna Booher

THE PRINTED WORD

FILING TIPS

The world is full of people suffering from severe cases of terminal piles. Everything ends up piled. Nothing ends up filed.

To get and keep your filing system working for you, follow these guidelines.

Be consistent with your labelling. Typed labels look neater than handwritten ones. However, titles written in black with a medium-tip felt pen are easier to read. If your filing backs up as you wait to type labels, you'll find it easier to keep up if you print the titles by hand.

Keep file titles brief. Use two or three words at most. Always begin with the noun – not an adjective.

Color coding can help you locate files more quickly and allow you to flag folders for special handling. A red file may contain letters awaiting signature or red files could be used for all active projects.

Use color with care. If your system becomes overly complicated (special colored inks on special colored labels on special colored folders), you'll spend too much time searching for the right colors.

File on a regular basis. Digging repeatedly through the "To File" pile wastes time. Set aside a few minutes every day or every week to tackle the filing.

Before you head to the filing cabinet, sort the papers to be filed to match the rough order of your system. This avoids having to move back and forth between and within file drawers.

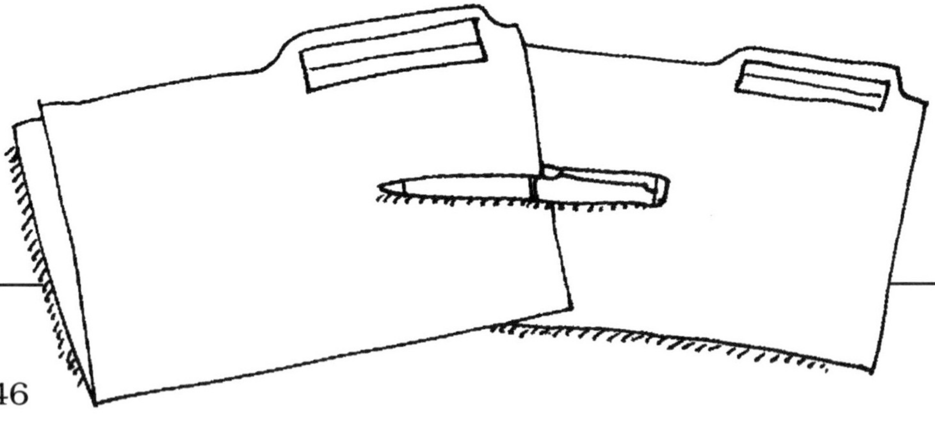

Staple papers together before filing. Don't use paper clips. They grab other stray papers and lead to "missing-in-action" searches.

Cut down on repeat decision making. Note the file reference name or number in pencil on the top right corner of documents as they move in to or out of a file.

File the most recent paper on the top of the stack in each file.

As you close or work with files, toss papers that are no longer useful.

To unclutter active file areas, note discard and archive dates on file tabs.

Identify master copies of forms and documents, so that you don't give away your last copy. Cross reference master copies to computer files containing the original document or data.

If files keep disappearing without a trace, start an Out-File system. Purchase inserts from a stationery store or make your own stand-up cards. Replace files that are removed with an Out card on which is noted the date and the name of the borrower.

Subdivide files before they show signs of strain. When you've accumulated more than an inch of loose papers in one file or if you're spending a lot of time searching through the file, it's time to subdivide the material into several folders.

Avoid paper cuts and mangled folders. Don't overcrowd file drawers. Leave two to four inches of free space in each drawer.

Stick a label on the front of each file drawer to highlight its contents.

Write a description of your filing system so that your colleagues, your replacement or temporary help can easily understand the setup.

And finally, before filing, scrutinize each piece of paper and ask whether it deserves to be kept at all.

"If you file it, you'll know where it is but you'll never need it. If you don't file it, you'll need it, but never know where it is."

Tillis' Organizational Principle

THE PRINTED WORD

CARD TRICKS

You pick them up everywhere – at meetings, shops, businesses, and trade shows. They're not just tiny pieces of cardboard. They're contacts, leads, future friends, business associates and clients.

Business cards pave the way for follow-up and future contact. There is a real art to handling them with finesse.

Carry cards wherever you go. You never know when the person with whom you share a ten-minute conversation in the line-up at the football game might be someone that you want to contact later.

Avoid handing out dog-eared crumpled cards by carrying them in a business card holder. Choose a container that doesn't require a lot of fumbling to get access to the cards. Don't stuff it so full that the contents explode all over the floor when you finally tug one card loose.

Think carefully about the design of your business card. Your choice of paper, ink color, type style and visuals all convey an image of your business.

Make sure the text on your cards is easy to read. Scrolling italics may be pretty but are tough to decipher. A brief description of your business or your business slogan will add promotional value to your card.

Consider the more subtle messages, too. When you include your telephone area code and country, you telegraph that your market is national or international in scope. When you list your home phone number on a business card you suggest that you are available to clients outside of regular business hours.

Be consistent about where you tuck the cards you pick up during the course of a regular business day or at a conference. Pick a pocket and develop the habit of unloading it regularly.

If you record a reminder or another person's address on the back of your own business card, draw a line through the information on the front so you don't accidentally give the card away to someone else.

When you receive someone else's card, record key information on the flip side. Note the date and year you picked up the card, where you met the person, and something about his or her business specialty.

Add a brief description that will help you recall the person or your conversation: she had a bad case of laryngitis, we shared lunch at Booglianni's Restaurant, he's the father of six daughters.

New contact information is most easily retrieved when it is integrated into your regular system for tracking names and addresses.

If you use a Rolodex, a guide-rail punch is available for notching the cards. Or look for self adhesive plastic tabs with notched rail guides. You simply press the sticky half of the tab along the bottom edge of the business card and pop the card onto the Rolodex. The adhesive strip is clear so all information shows through.

Some people staple business cards directly to their full-size Rolodex cards. An alternate approach is to add plastic covers to the Rolodex cards and slide the business cards in the see-through pocket. Extra cards can be tucked in behind to be given away as required.

When someone offers you a business card, you may wish to ask for several copies. Add one to your own office Rolodex, another to the general office Rolodex and tape the third card inside the front cover of his client or vendor file folder for quick and easy reference. Or if your memory is unreliable, you may want to file one card under the person's surname and a second card under the name of the business.

Don't feel pressured to save every card you receive. Some will be leads or contacts that you have no intention of following up. Toss them immediately. Don't cram your system with extraneous information.

Do check out electronic contact management software. Its greatest advantage is that you can search by any descriptor from business name to personal name to city. Relieves a lot of the pressure on the old memory bank!

THE PRINTED WORD

For your information

Great intentions! That's what many of us experience when we pack up an armload of reading material to catch up on over the weekend or on vacation.

A recent retiree reported that she had planned for years to catch up on her reading once she retired. It's not working out. In retirement, she now has even more time to browse through libraries and bookstores, picking up new titles. She's losing ground.

It's tough to keep up, at home and at the office, with a growing stack of magazines, journals and clippings. These suggestions may help.

The sheer size of a stack of reading material can stop you from digging in. Try tackling it in small pieces. Spend one hour in the library reading room as a reward for finishing a project. Build 15 minutes of reading time into the least productive part of your day when your energy is especially low. Take a journal and a cup of coffee out of the office for a midafternoon break.

Improve your reading speed through special training. Learn to scan headlines and the opening paragraphs of articles. Use the table of contents to select the most useful and interesting articles.

Build reading into other activities. Reading while riding a stationary exercise bike can make the miles and pages fly by quite painlessly.

Limit what you add to your reading pile. Choose one or two key topics on which you want to be better informed.

Concentrate on articles and books relating to those issues for a few months.

If you have studied a particular topic for a long time, you may have outgrown the editorial level of some publications. New books in any given field won't always offer new ideas. They may be a rehash of information you already have. If a quick scan reveals no new insights, move on to something else.

Take your name off circulation lists and cancel subscriptions for publications you don't read. Consider how much of your time you can realistically devote to reading. One organizational seminar participant reported that her five-member household subscribed to a total of 32 monthly publications. Yikes!

Make "to save" decisions on your first read. Write the page numbers to be clipped on the cover of the magazine. Paper clip or turn over the corners of pages to be saved. If the journal is in circulation, add a space to the routing slip for readers to note pages to be clipped or copied at the end of the route. Share the task of keeping up. Deal out the journals for the month amongst your co-workers and take turns bringing each other up to date at staff meetings.

If your office has the financial resources, hire a clipping service to scan the papers and journals on your behalf. You identify the key issues and topics on which you wish to be kept informed. The service provides you with a weekly or monthly collection of articles on those subjects (and a bill for the service, of course).

Take advantage of audio and video cassettes. Taped summaries of new business books are available by subscription. Audiotapes are portable and easily combined with other activities.

Jump the reading ruts occasionally. Try something from an entirely different field of interest. You may find ideas that, when applied to your own situation, offer a whole new perspective on problems and opportunities.

THE PRINTED WORD

NEWSLETTER KNOW-HOW

Many organizations rely on a newsletter to keep their members informed and involved. Businesses use newsletters to establish credibility, inform clients and generate more business. Asssociations use newsletters to promote their interests to outside groups.

But if your newsletter doesn't get read, it's not doing any of these jobs.

You need to get people reading and you need to keep them reading. These tips will help.

Design an eye-catching masthead for your publication. It should be simple, clear, unique and readily associated with your group.

Concentrate on designing an attractive and interesting front page. Color helps, but it's not critical. Design and layout are more important.

Check out the resources at your local print shop. They'll be able to tell you about the most effective, least-expensive print techniques.

Highlight the benefits of reading the newsletter right up front. Let your readers know why they should turn the page. Check out the magazine covers on any newstand for great ideas on teaser titles.

Be brief. People read newsletters that are short and to the point. Most readers will scan a one-page newsletter (even one that is printed both sides) when it first hits the desk or pops out of the mailbox. Longer editions are set aside for later and more apt to be lost in the shuffle.

Keep your articles short. You're publishing a newsletter not a magazine.

Create lots of white space between blocks of text. If the piece is too heavy on the ink, readers will be discouraged.

Short quips, quotes and cartoons grab attention and draw people through the material. Choose humor that relates to the organization or to the subject of a featured article.

Write for a low-reading grade level. Keep your sentences short. Use simple words.

Get personal. Play up the people in your organization. Use names and pictures.

Aim for a quality product. In these days of computers, desktop publishing programs and quality copiers, readers expect crisp, clean copy. There's no excuse for smudges and smears.

Get the beast out on time – that's before "Upcoming Events" turns into "Last Month's News".

It's far better to send a short newsletter on time than a full-length edition two weeks late. Set a publication schedule to keep yourself on track.

"It is better to be brief than tedious."

William Shakespeare

KEEPING IN TOUCH

PHONE MASTERY

What has twelve buttons, comes in all shapes and colors, speaks with a shrill and insistent voice, and specializes in interruptions? Your telephone, of course!

Telephone interruptions and telephone tag can drive you to distraction. But phone calls are not always timewasters or interruptions; they are important links to customers, family and friends.

Despite all the difficulties in connecting by phone, it's still more economical than driving across town or flying halfway around the world.

Here are some things you can do to make your phone work for you.

Place your phone in the proper spot so the handset cord doesn't stretch across your writing area.

Attach a long cord or switch to a portable to give you greater mobility. While you are waiting on hold or listening to a long story, you can polish off a couple of odd jobs. A shoulder rest or a headset will free up your hands for note taking.

Group phone calls and place several at the same time. This cuts down on the number of times you go through the "getting ready" process – clearing a path to the phone, pulling out the phone book, locating pen and notepaper.

Organize your thoughts and pull all the information you need before you start dialing. If you are calling to set a meeting date, have your calendar at hand. If you are passing along information, set your notes in front of you.

If you are dialing your way through a long list of calls, note the name of the person you are calling as you dial. This avoids that long embarrassed silence that occurs when someone finally answers and you can't remember who you've just called.

Be prepared to leave a useful callback message. A detailed message helps the other person return your call with the necessary information on hand at a time when you are most likely to be available.

Speak fast when a receptionist announces that you will be put on hold. If you are calling long distance, say so. If you don't want to be put on hold, leave a brief message or say you will call back later.

If you choose to linger on hold, use your speaker feature. Switch to the hands-free line, turn up the volume and go about your business until the person you are calling comes on line.

When the phone that rings is yours, don't wait for a second or third notice. Answer on the first ring. Your concentration has already been broken.

If the phone calls as you are rushing out the door to an appointment, let it ring. Don't let the twelve-button monster make you late.

To keep calls brief and to the point, be businesslike from the start. Don't ask, "How are you today?" It's a question that invites a long and detailed response.

Try this opening: "Sam, it's good to hear from you. What can I do for you today?" It's friendly and moves the caller directly to the purpose of the call.

Use your phone to save time, gas and parking money. Check to see if the dentist is running late, the plane is on time, or the warehouse is open. Confirm that the work you plan to pick up is finished. Call to see if the store carries the item you want. While you have the clerk on the line, check on the price and ask whether the item is in stock.

If you find yourself tied up in unwanted phone solicitations, say, "No thank you!" or "We're not interested!" Then simply hang up the phone. You don't need to feel awkward about interrupting the solicitor's chatty buildup to the sales pitch. After all, the caller interrupted you.

You can't be held hostage by your own telephone unless you are a willing accomplice. It takes two people to keep a call alive.

KEEPING IN TOUCH

CELLULAR ETIQUETTE

Snapshot #1: *So there we were – a dozen of us – waiting in line to pay our lunch tabs. Standing in front of me was Mr. Cellular, portable phone glued to his ear, voice raised to make himself heard over the lunchtime din.*

Snapshot #2: *So there they were – an associate and her family – queued up for the next ride at Disneyland. Standing in front of them was Mr. Cellular, instructing his broker to buy this, sell that and hold onto something else. The business talk burst the holiday bubble, turning their thoughts immediately to their businesses back home.*

Snapshot #3: *So there they were – an entire theatre audience. At a moment of high drama, the phone rang. Mr. Cellular, seated in the audience, not only answered the call, he conducted the conversation on the spot.*

The cellular portable telephone is a wonderful tool. It allows realtors, sales reps., construction managers and small business owners to conduct business on the move. It eliminates the search for a public telephone. Cellular phones offer security in the face of travel emergencies. They provide peace of mind for on-the-go parents who want to be accessible to their children.

However, in the hands of the unconscious and inconsiderate user, the portable phone becomes a public nuisance.

Phone conversations are considered a private matter. Being a party to a public phone conversation can leave bystanders feeling uncomfortable – as if they are the ones who are intruding on a private moment. Respect those feelings and minimize your intrusions.

Turn your telephone off when attending events that ought not to be disturbed by the ringing of a phone. Concerts, theatre performances, church services, weddings and special dinners all fall into that category.

Consider other options if you must know when someone is trying to reach you. Choose a cellular phone that allows you to turn off the ringer, but leaves you with a visual call indicator (like a flashing keypad or signal light). Pick up your phone and move to a more appropriate spot to answer the call. Think about subscribing to a cellular messaging or paging service.

When you do take a call in a public place, be considerate. Keep the call short and your voice low.

For longer calls, remove yourself from the main public areas to a more suitable service area (e.g., hallway, entryway or washroom).

If the timing or location is inappropriate, indicate this to your caller and offer to call back (e.g., from your parked car when dinner is over).

Be concerned for the comfort of your immediate companions and the general public seated around you.

Ask other portable phone users how they deal with situations. Ask friends and colleagues who don't use portable phones for their reactions and suggestions.

Check with your cellular telephone dealer. The companies, themselves, recognize that thoughtless users create both image problems and accidents. Look to their newsletters for information on cellular etiquette.

"There is more to life than increasing its speed."
Mhatma Gandhi

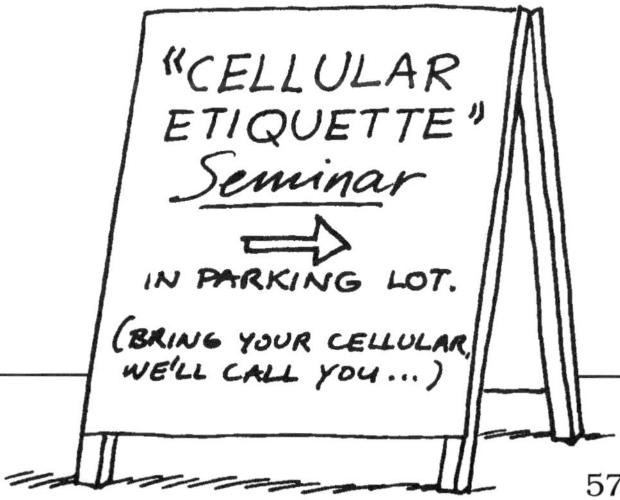

KEEPING IN TOUCH

CONFERENCE CALLS

Would you like to spend fewer hours in meetings, travel less and cut down on expenses? Try meeting by phone. It's the only meeting at which all members make their own coffee and there are no arguments about where to go for lunch!

Conference calls are most appropriate when you are trying to pass along the same message to all members of your group, collect opinions and advice on a specific issue, pool information or check progress on previously made plans.

Conference calls fall short when you are trying to build relationships and make connections between participants who do not know each other very well. It's also tough to debate emotional issues, plan complex activities and make complicated decisions by phone.

Advance planning is critical for a successful conference call.

If you are convening the call, be sure to send out a specific agenda in advance. Indicate start and end times for the meeting (include time-zone information if appropriate). Specify who will take the lead or provide the detail for each item.

Include essential background information with the agenda. Don't try to describe graphs, diagrams or budget numbers over the phone.

Confirm the participation of all parties a day or two before the call itself. Your Conference Operator will do this for you.

Gather all materials and information you will need for the call before your phone rings. Hang a "Call-In-Progress – Do-Not-

Disturb" sign on your door or book yourself into a vacant conference room for the call.

Begin the conference with a roll call. If anyone's reception or outgoing sound is poor, suggest that person try another extension.

Review the agenda and set the ground rules for the call. Describe what you expect by way of participation. Remind participants to be concise in their comments, and that you can't see them nod in agreement or shake their heads. All reactions will need to be verbal.

If group members are not all that well-acquainted, suggest that they preface their comments with their names. A simple "Pat, here" will help everyone keep track of who is speaking.

Be aware of background sounds during your call (phones, printers, rustling papers). Keep them to a minimum. Avoid side conversations.

Watch your mannerisms. Don't chew gum; avoid breathing directly into the sensitive mouthpiece. Swing the handset under your chin or up to the top of your head, or hit the "Mute" button while you are not talking.

Smile. It adds warmth to your voice. Sit up straight or stand if you wish. More air in your diaphragm means better voice control.

Take notes. It will help you concentrate. If you need to provide a written summary of the discussion, you may want to record the call (with the permission of the participants).

Visualize others as they are speaking. If you are meeting with your staff or Board Members, prop a photo of the group in front of you or duplicate it on the top of the agenda for everyone's reference.

Pay attention to the tone and forcefulness of the voices you are hearing. You'll receive a more complete message than if you simply listen to the words.

Summarize constantly and check for understanding and agreement as you go.

Add a little humor. Laughter is just as effective by phone as it is in person.

"Meetings are like funerals. Both are a gathering of people who are wearing uncomfortable clothing and would rather be somewhere else."

Dave Barry

KEEPING IN TOUCH

GETTING TO KNOW YOU

Successful organizations use their people resources well. Does yours?

Much of the energy that drives organizations is generated when people connect with one other. It's when you make those connections that you commit to helping each other, and begin to plug in your ideas and resources. That's when the creative sparks start to fly!

To build that commitment and stoke that fire, you'll need to crank up the information exchange and learn as much as possible about each person's resources, talents and abilities.

How much do you really know about the people in your group? What skills do they have to offer? What skills are they hoping to develop further?

What kinds of education and training have they had? What do they feel comfortable teaching others?

What kinds of experiences and responsibilities have they had with other organizations? What did they like/dislike about that involvement?

At what stage is their family? What hobbies and special interests excite them?

What kinds of resources (equipment, support services, information, personal contacts) can they access?

What piqued their interest in this kind of work? In what areas would they like to be involved? What are they hoping to get from their involvement?

These techniques will help you share this kind of information.

Complete annual profile sheets – from scratch for new members – with updates for long-term group members.

Post the resource profiles (complete with photos) at your annual planning meeting. Give each member of the group a set of profiles. Suggest ways they might make use of the information.

Profile one or two members in each newsletter or at the beginning of each meeting.

Research a set of trivia questions about the people you are working with. Toss in a few questions between agenda items at your meetings.

Share information about different areas (e.g., previous work experiences or access to resources) as a regular part of each meeting.

Plan a few informal activities for your meetings. Ask group members to wear hats, pins or T-shirts from past work lives, or to bring along books that represent special interests. Props promote a relaxed exchange of experiences and are great visual memory cues.

Even if you're an experienced member of an organization and have worked alongside other members for years, never assume that you know everything about their interests or capabilities.

Be alert to changes. Ask what's new or what's different since the last time you were together ...

"Communications help to keep people feeling included in and connected to the organization ... give people information, and do it again and again."
William Bridges

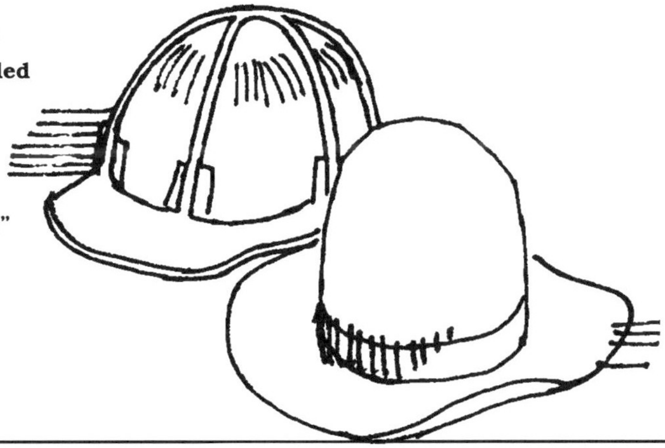

KEEPING IN TOUCH

THE KNACK OF NETWORKING

So there you are – on your own – in the midst of a room of strangers. You made the decision to get out there and meet new people. You joined a community group or a business association. You're attending your first event and you don't know a soul. Now what?

A recent poll billed "attending an event with strangers" as the most uncomfortable life situation (with good old public speaking relegated to number two on the list).

If you are new to the networking scene, these tips will help you relax.

To ease your way into opening a conversation, plan and practice a ten second self introduction. Start with a brief description of what you do and conclude with your name and business. This approach gives the listener time to tune in and provides an interesting peg on which to hang your name.

A comment that establishes what you have in common with other attendees at the event might help open the conversation. (e.g., "This is my first visit to this group. Are you a member?")

Think of yourself as a host rather than a guest. Look for ways to put others at ease by opening conversations and introducing those you meet to those you know.

Go into an event with two or three pieces of "small talk" in mind. These are openers for light conversations you could have with anyone. An opener might be a statement, a question, or an interesting experience. Draw from current events, personal interests, humorous stories, travels, or personal adventures of the day.

Ask questions of the people you meet and demonstrate a real interest in their answers. Listen carefully. Give the other person your full attention.

If you've met someone before, but forgotten the other person's name, say so. Offer your own name in introduction. You will see puzzled expressions disappear on other people's faces as you relieve them of the need to struggle with memory searches of their own.

Keep circulating – don't get stuck in one location or conversation. If you have trouble closing a conversation and moving on, be direct. Finish a comment and simply say, "Excuse me, it was nice meeting you." Then move to another part of the room.

Be cautious about your personal habits. Smoking and drinking to excess will cause you problems.

Guard against that phony friendliness that has given networking a bad name – looking over people's shoulders, shaking hands just to pass along a business card, checking out name tags and titles searching for people who can "do something for you", and not making good on promises or offers of help and information. This kind of behavior will not turn strangers into friends or clients.

Building and maintaining relationships is an ongoing process. Touch base with others on a regular basis, not just when you need a favor.

Demanding or expecting leads, information and support, just because you have connected with someone, is way out of line.

Reciprocity is important. A pattern of always giving or always taking creates an awkward imbalance.

Acknowledge all forms of support you receive from others – including gifts of time, favors, leads and ideas. A personalized thank you is always appropriate.

"The aim of small talk is to make people comfortable – to put them at their ease – not to teach, preach or impress."

Sir Alexander Korda

HI-TECH HOW-TO

ELECTRONIC MESSAGING

With a mighty Internet Hi Ho another electronic message sails bravely into cyberspace.

E-mail (the electronic pony express) is so easy to use that for many individuals it outranks the phone and fax as their communication tool of choice.

There are ways to make this electronic invention even more effective.

Pay close attention to the titling of your message. A short but informative subject description pays off. If it's a sales teaser, a great subject line may encourage the receiver to open your letter first.

A clear title helps the receiver recall the contents after a message has been read and "tucked back in its envelope". An informative title helps the receiver file the message in the appropriate place – for future action or reference.

It's so easy to distribute multiple copies of electronic messages that users are often tempted to copy anyone who might have shown even the barest glimmer of interest in a subject. This approach plugs the electronic mailboxes of colleagues with junk information that must be read, sorted, dumped and filed by all.

Instead of firing off 20 copies at the touch of a key, imagine yourself photocopying the document and personally delivering individual copies. If you wouldn't make the effort to deliver it by other means, don't send it by E-Mail.

Learn the shortcuts. Use a reply button to send a message back to your correspondent. No need to look up or retype return addresses – the software handles it for you.

Discover how your E-mail software might be customized for your use. Learn how to set up distribution groupings for convenient bulk mailing to working teams.

Personalize any signature file that may appear at the end of your messages to promote a new product, reinforce your business focus, or provide complete contact information to the receiver.

Most E-Mail systems allow you to indicate the priority level of messages – from Regular to Urgent, or Special Attention. A priority system will only work if all users respect the designations. Once users start marking every message “Urgent”, the system is sunk.

You probably wouldn’t appreciate someone popping into your office every 5 minutes repeatedly interrupting your focus on the task at hand. You may wish to set up your E-Mail system so it doesn’t visibly or audibly interrupt you while you are working on priority projects.

Locate the “switch” for the visual or audible alarms that indicate you’ve just received more mail on line. Turn it off during those times when you don’t want to be interrupted. You may be able to instruct your system to routinely check for mail at start-up or at certain intervals through the day rather than having it delivered as it arrives.

Set up Action Files to handle your incoming E-Mail in the same way you would handle the paperwork that lands on your desk. Pop an E-Mail letter into a Waiting-For-Callback file when you leave a message and are waiting for the receiver to call back.

Coordinate your electronic and paper action files so you only need remember one set of titles. An archive file will give you a chronological record of incoming and outgoing messages.

Watch the tone and content of your E-Mail conversations. Take a moment to review your notes before you send them on their way. Keep it respectful. Keep it professional. E-mail is not the route to use to advertise your frustrations or your garage sale.

Always bear in mind that E-Mail is neither a secure nor private form of communication. Correspond accordingly.

“My sources are unreliable, but

their information is fascinating.”

Ashleigh Brilliant

ORGANIZING COMPUTER FILES

If you're worried that your Mac is about to DOS its cookies, and you've no idea what's already hit the trash, you're not alone. Files sink out of sight just as fast on a hard drive as they do in a twelve-drawer bank of paper files.

Don't despair. There are successful ways to organize administrative information and work in progress.

One point about which all sources are clear is the need to subdivide your information. Trying to operate with only one directory or one huge file is like dumping all your loose papers into a giant collection bin and sending someone to sort through it all each time you need something specific.

Start by separating applications (the tools) from the data files (the products) you create. For example, keep the letters and memos you write with your word processing program separate from the software itself.

This makes it easier to create backups of documents without having to back up your programs each time. It also helps avoid the problem of accidentally deleting a program file, thinking it was just an old memo or letter that deserved to hit the trash.

Take a close look at how your paper files are organized. If the paper system is working and makes sense to you, build your computer files in parallel. Depending on your type of business, you might set up separate electronic "file drawers" or directories for Clients, General Administration, Lists, Projects, Personnel, Departments, Associations, Marketing, Finance, Suppliers, etc.

Within each directory, create sub-directories as required. For example, each Client might have his or her own file. When searching through one client's documents begins to take too long, create sub-files for that client labeled Correspondence, Contracts, Projects, etc.

Another useful approach is to create the files you will need for each project before the activity begins. You may know from past experience that each team project generates these types of materials and documents: Proposals, Project Plans, Meeting Agendas & Minutes, Progress Reports, Correspondence, Contracts, Budgets & Financial Statements. Set up all of these files at the outset and file the documents appropriately as they are created.

Name your documents in a consistent and meaningful way. Some systems are more limiting than others when it comes to naming – making it even more important to be concise and consistent. Depending on your system, you will likely have somewhere between 11 and 31 characters with which to name each item.

Use numbers or letters in certain positions as symbols. For example, the first character might indicate the type of document. M=Memo, L=Letter, C=Contract, R=Report, and so on. The numbers 1-4 could replace letters and serve the same purpose.

When you create successive versions of the same information, borrow an idea from software companies who indicate progressive releases with number extensions (Rep-McMillan.1, Rep-McMillan.2, etc.)

Consistency in naming makes it easier to use the built in features of your system to search for lost files. If you can remember that you wrote a letter on Friday, chances are pretty good that your search function will be able to quickly locate all letters written that particular day.

Having trouble locating the electronic version of the paper in your hand? You may be interested in an option that allows you to "brand" your document by printing the document name and directory path in very small lettering as part of the footer on each printed page. Think of it as a mini-road map for retracing your steps when the bread crumbs in the forest have completely disappeared.

"As with any technology, if you just automate sloppy personal habits and disorganized files, you'll just mess things up faster."

Jim Clemmer

HI-TECH HOW-TO

JUST THE FAX, MA'AM!

Fax machines have changed the pace of business life. Not long ago, correspondence by post was the norm.

But today, if you haven't had a noon reply to a 10:00 a.m. fax, you're on the phone to find out what's wrong with those folks at the other end.

Pressure? You bet! Progress? Not necessarily!

Fax machines and computer fax modems are wonderful tools; but they're no excuse for poor planning! Just because you've left something to the last minute is no reason someone else should have to take the heat!

A quick response may be appreciated. But hurriedly faxed copies of promotional materials – with misfed pages and crooked margins – don't do much for your business image.

And, a speedy response may not always be the wisest choice. It takes time to think things through – to consider options, to generate sound solutions to complex problems. Occasionally, it's better to bypass the fax and take your time.

That said, here are a few tips for those times when the fax is the best choice for the job.

Cut some slack for the folks on the receiving end of your messages. Instant transmission doesn't guarantee instant reception.

Not everyone dashes to catch the latest fax as it churns out of the machine. In larger organizations, faxes may arrive in a central location and only be delivered once a day. People travel, take holidays and work on other priorities.

Allow a reasonable amount of time for a response. Avoid asking for a reply by "return fax" unless it's absolutely necessary.

Collect samples of your own fax transmissions. Check the quality of the copy that appears at the other end. Some of what you see relates to the quality of the receiving machine – but the originating equipment plays a big part in the equation!

Check the accuracy of the information that appears on the header line of your transmissions. You don't want to slip a digit and send out the wrong phone number at the top of every fax.

When possible, delay transmissions to take advantage of cheaper long-distance rates during off-hours.

Add a fax modem to your computer. Transmissions are cleaner because you skip a step in the process. The documents don't have to be printed and fed through the stand-alone fax.

With a fax modem, you can receive a fax, read it on screen, and destroy it or reroute it to someone else without ever having to print a paper copy. Less filing and piling!

Scan your signature, store it in your computer scrapbook, and pop it into faxable memos and letters that are generated using your word processor.

Experiment with the broadcast function on your regular fax or on your fax modem. This allows you to send the same information to several people without feeding or redirecting the same document over and over again.

Broadcasting is great for distributing the minutes of business meetings. No more printing, copying, stuffing of envelopes and licking of stamps! The fax modem takes care of all those steps and sends the same minutes to all participants with one simple command.

"Time is that quality of nature that keeps events from happening all at once. Lately it doesn't seem to be working."

Annonymous

HI-TECH HOW-TO

IS THAT YOUR VOICE IN THE MAIL?

If you've ever placed what you thought was going to be a simple phone call and ended up being taken hostage by the phone system at the other end, you've had first-hand experience with voice mail hell. In fact, it could be that as you read this, you are still on hold waiting for an option that appeals to you enough to press a number on the keypad.

Voice mail systems, also known as message managers, were meant to take the place of answering machines and overloaded receptionists. Many systems have only succeeded in creating frustrated callers. But there are ways to make this technology work for you.

If you expect to be calling the same place of business frequently, take notes on the sequence of numbers and options that are offered the first time you make a call. You'll be able to punch your way through the maze more quickly on subsequent calls without having to wait for an explanation of menu choices.

When you encounter voice mail, leave a detailed message that will allow the other person to call back with an informed response to your questions. Cue that person as to the best time to reach you or indicate that he or she can call and leave a message with the information you've requested.

When it's your own system, create an answering message that is helpful for the caller. Vague messages are frustrating. "I'm either on the phone, out of the office, or on holidays," is pretty limited information.

Update the message to make it as specific as possible. "It's Tuesday, the 21st, and I'm out of the office at a sales Conference until the 23rd. I'll be returning phone calls on Thursday afternoon."

With a message like this, the caller can make an informed decision about his or her next step and have a clear idea as to when he or she is likely to hear from you.

Keep the advertising to a minimum. Your caller is not going to want to be paying the long distance charges to listen to you recount the specials of the day.

If you are designing your system, remember that caller-friendly voice mail gives the caller an immediate opportunity to cut through the recorded message to speak directly with a live person. "Press '0' to speak with my secretary," is one of the most welcome options on any voice mail menu.

When you offer the caller a menu of possibilities, keep the choices to a minimum. Never put the caller in a catch 22 situation – a voice mail tree that works the caller into the position of not being able to get out of a loop.

Investigate voice mail system options. Can it be set to automatically roll the line over to another person rather than the message manager? This could be a better way to handle inquiries where several people are in a position to field the same kind of question.

Are you wondering how your recorded message and voice mail system are being received by your callers? Call up a few folks and ask their opinions. Or you could always turn your survey into another menu choice: "To let us know what you think of our voice mail service, press 7." You'll no doubt get a few opinions!

"His phone is busy. His voice mail is busy. His fax is busy, and his modem is busy. I think I'll just walk over and talk to him."

Overheard in hallway by Chris Hoover

TRANSIT TIPS

UP, UP AND AWAY!

Are tiny packets of airline peanuts falling out of your briefcase and coat pockets at every turn?

Are you reciting the preflight safety spiel in your sleep?

When "Leaving on a jet plane – don't know when I'll be back again", becomes your personal theme song, you know you are chalking up the big airmiles. These transit tips will come in handy.

Develop an ongoing relationship with a professional travel counselor. A full-service agency will maintain a complete travel information file, cutting down on the number of times you have to repeat those basic details: address, phone and fax numbers, credit card numbers, frequent flyer plan numbers, and preferences in airlines and seating arrangements.

Learn as much as possible about the airlines and airports that you use most often. Check out your options – especially when you are traveling free of check-in baggage.

Can you arrange to have boarding passes issued in advance along with your ticket and completely bypass the check-in lineups at the terminal? Can you pass through security with just a show of your ticket and pick up your boarding pass at the gate?

When you have work to do and time to spare before your flight, go through security early (before preflight line-ups form) and settle down in the departure lounge. You'll end up with a larger block of time than if you settle down in the general waiting area, unpack your work, pack up to move through security, and unpack a second time to work again in the departure lounge.

Moving through security on arrival also helps you bypass those log jams that occur when a class of 30 exchange students or the entire junior hockey team shows up 15 minutes before flight time.

Do what you can to lighten up! Invest in lightweight luggage and a lightweight briefcase. The papers, clothes and accessories you pack are heavy enough on their own. You don't want cases that weigh a lot when empty.

If your travel includes quick trips and short hauls, a garment bag makes more sense than a suitcase. You'll end up doing less folding, unfolding and pressing – at both ends of your trip.

Garment bags are usually welcomed as carry-on luggage. Some flights offer convenient do-it-yourself valet service. Drop your garment bag on the cart as you board the plane; pick it up on your way off the plane at your destination.

Don't drag an overstuffed garment bag into the cabin of the plane. Even though cabin storage compartments are more spacious these days, your fellow passengers won't appreciate having to lean out of the way as you drag the bag down the aisle and hoist it over your head into the overhead bin. Heavy cases pose less of a safety risk when stored below in cargo bays than when they are jammed into the cabin area.

A saddle-bag suitcase that wraps around a standard briefcase is a great travel option for those who are able to pack compactly for overnight trips. This four-pocket unit slides over the handle and buckles around the ends of the briefcase. Presto! Only one bag to carry!

Always tuck a copy of your itinerary in your suitcase. If your baggage goes astray for a few days, it could help the carrier track you down.

"We're not lost. We're locationally challenged."

John M. Ford

TRANSIT TIPS

DINING ON THE RUN

When you're out for a fine dining experience, then the meal itself is the event! You've got all the time in the world to wait for a table, relax between courses and linger over coffee.

But if you are grabbing breakfast enroute to the plane, sandwiching a quick lunch between meetings or riding herd on restless youngsters, you need a fast meal.

Try these approaches for speedy service.

Schedule your meals for off-times – either later or earlier than the main crowd. Some restaurants offer early-bird-specials for patrons who arrive before the evening rush hour.

Call ahead for lunch and dinner reservations, especially if your group is large. This allows the restaurant staff to set up the right number of place settings so your table is ready when you arrive.

Think about what you would like to eat as you make your way to the restaurant. Many restaurant menus (especially breakfast ones) are similar. If you know what you want, you can bypass a look at the menu and place your order at the time you are seated.

Let your waiter know if you are in a hurry. Be specific. Explain what time you need to be on your way and ask if that is realistic.

Treat your waiter/waitress with courtesy. "Heh, Bud!" hollered across a crowded dining room will not improve your chances for attentive service.

Stick with standard fare. Special orders (a little more of this ... a little less of that ... substitutions ... something on the side) often take longer to prepare. Salad bars, buffets and specials-of-the-day are usually your quickest options.

Will members of your group need separate checks? Tell the waitress when you make your reservation and reconfirm when you place your order.

Do you need a receipt for business purposes? Let the cashier know before your charges are entered in the cash register.

Staying in a hotel? Avoid the breakfast rush completely by using room service. Call in your breakfast order the night before. When you do eat in the hotel restaurant, side-step check-out line-ups by signing the bill over to your room. Simply drop it with the cashier on your way out.

Unsure about whether a restaurant is right for your crowd, your timetable or your pocketbook? Take a peek inside and ask to see a menu. The decor, the clientele and the prices will all help you make your decision.

Travelling on a tight schedule with a restless crew of youngsters? Search for a restaurant with some nearby open space. Seat yourselves and place your orders. While one family member holds down the table, another can take the little ones outside for five or ten minutes to run off excess energy.

When a waiter or waitress has been especially accommodating, share the praise and tip accordingly.

Expect good food and good service. If your milk or coffee creamer is sour, say so. Don't just stew about it! Speak up. Give your hosts a chance to please you. After all, they are in the hospitality business.

"For fast-acting relief, try slowing down."

Lily Tomlin

TRANSIT TIPS

HOTEL KNOW-HOW

For frequent travellers, hotel rooms are the next best thing to home. Take note of these travel tips for greater comfort and fewer hassles.

If you'll be staying at a hotel that's new to you, find out about the services and facilities when you make your reservation.

Indicate your special needs. If you love to swim but hate dripping your way through the hallways, ask for a room close to the pool.

If you will be attending a large conference, ask for a room on one of the lower levels. When you are only one or two floors up from the conference area, you can shortcircuit elevator line-ups and get your exercise on the stairs.

If you plan to make a lot of phone calls from your room, inquire about service charges. Some hotels place a timed surcharge on all calls made through the switchboard, even though you reverse the charges or use your calling card.

Plan ahead to make your stay more hospitable. Pack a travel coffee perk. Stash snack items in your suitcase. Take along a family photo or a favorite book.

Carry plenty of change. Quarters and dollars are handy for tips and phone calls.

Tuck your hotel reservation confirmation number in your wallet or keep it with your airline ticket. You don't want to unpack your suitcase in the lobby, searching for proof of your reservation.

On your arrival, side-step long line-ups at the registration desk. Leave your bags with the bellhop and check in later. Detour to the newsstand for a paper, make a couple of phone calls or have a quick snack.

Be prepared to conduct as much business as possible when you register. If you won't be toting up extra charges, pay for your room in advance. If you would like to arrange an extended checkout time, ask now.

Hang up your clothes soon after you settle in. Some travel wrinkles will disappear after a few hours on a hanger.

Check the literature in your room for useful information – maps, transit information, tourist suggestions.

Take advantage of other hotel information services. Ask for restaurant suggestions, store hours information or the location of the nearest pharmacy. Why head ten blocks east when the shop you need is only one block west?

The hotel staff can advise you on airport shuttle bus services as well. Be sure to indicate your flight departure time. A 20-minute trip to the airport in the middle of the afternoon can easily stretch to 40 minutes during rush hour.

Checking out in the morning? Note the length of the line-up as you head down for breakfast. If it seems short, check out before you eat.

Make it easy on yourself. Operating out of strange surroundings can be stressful enough, without the pressure of running late. Leave yourself extra time for everything – from elevator rides and cabs across town to meals and meetings.

When you receive great service, be as free with the compliments as you would be with complaints. Express your pleasure to the individual responsible. Better yet, take the person's name and send a written commendation to the individual and the hotel manager.

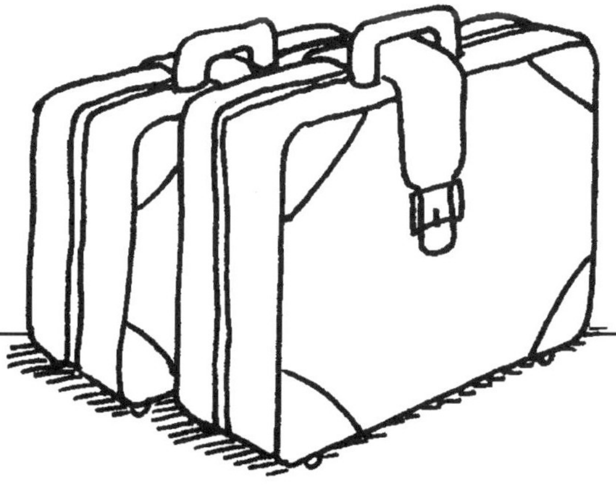

TRANSIT TIPS

THE MOBILE OFFICE

The driver's seat was originally designed with just one purpose in mind – navigation. When control central is turned into a launching pad for business meetings and presentations, a communications center for contact with the home office, and a mobile diner with snacks and meals "to go", it's a challenge to stay organized.

Number one rule: nail down the drinks! Outfit the dash or the "hump" with a unit that grips coffee cups and soft drinks, leaving your hands free. Life on the road is tough enough without trying to find a way to oust orange juice and coffee stains from clothes and brochures!

Unload the garbage at every opportunity. You don't collect empty pop cans, chip bags or dried-up orange peels in your everyday office, why do it on the road? Make "Gas In – Garbage Out" your janitorial motto.

Limit the number of extras you have up front at any time. If you listen to music or motivational tapes, choose a couple at the beginning of the day. Set the cassette carrying case in the back so that it's not cluttering up the front seat.

Devise a simple system for recording mileage and expenses. Designate one folder or envelope to hold receipts. Keep them close at hand. Recording as you go is much easier than trying to resurrect three-day-old numbers.

Don't leave loose papers and files lying around on the seats. Even normal braking and turning motions will send loose stacks of material into a free fall. An unexpected stop will catapult them to the floor. Belt in supply boxes or sample cases or set them on the floor.

If it makes sense for the kind of work you are doing, consider separating materials into several briefcases – one for calls and another for paperwork. Carry with you only what you will need for the activity at hand.

Sort materials according to the ways in which they will be used during calls, meetings or events. Set up a file box with dividers if you are handling many different forms, handouts or promotional materials.

If you will be moving materials in and out of the car, choose weatherproof containers rather than cardboard boxes. Vinyl cases or storage units can be set on the ground while you open the trunk or car door. Cardboard carriers disintegrate in the rain and snow.

Take a few minutes after each stop or event to note ideas, names, promises to forward information and other details while they are still fresh. Jot it all down in one spot – a steno pad, a loose-leaf binder, a notebook. Don't generate a minefield of notepapers, restaurant napkins and dead envelopes.

Spend time each evening organizing materials for the next day's commitments.

Set up an office supplies box that stays in your vehicle. Include a stapler, ruler, tape, extra pens, Post-It notes, stamps, and scissors. Add any other items that you use often (e.g., a small calculator). Store everything in a tool kit or tackle box. Replenish supplies at the end of every trip so the kit is always ready for action.

Since note taking and driving are not compatible activities, use a microcassette recorder to register inspirations before they disappear.

Think portable. An electronic diary that carries all the addresses and telephone numbers you need while on the road is less bulky than a more traditional address book. Cellular phones and laptop computers with fax modems make communication with the "home office" a breeze.

TRANSIT TIPS

HOLIDAY? WHAT HOLIDAY?

You work like a slave to get ready to go. You work like a slave to get caught up on your return. You know there's a holiday sandwiched somewhere in the middle.

Your calendar says you were away from the office. But with the double time you put in before and the triple time you put in after the fact, that restored, relaxed and refreshed vacation feeling doesn't last long – if it develops at all!

What to do to make it easier to get away and less of a shock to ease back into the harness? Practising self-defense can make all the difference.

Take a look at your workload in the weeks leading up to your departure date. Schedule activities and intermediate deadline dates that would get the most important efforts finished up a week or so before you are due to leave. That should provide some slack to handle last-minute emergencies and extended deadlines.

Give yourself a day or two of holiday time to get packed up. Working double time at the office and trying to pack and organize your trip at the same time only guarantees that you'll be exhausted when you start your holiday.

Ask a colleague or assistant to sort your mail and paperwork while you are away. Set up three holding files titled: For Immediate Attention, Important but Not Urgent and Rainy Day/Whenever!

Plan for part of your workload to be handled by others in your absence. Provide information and training. Delegate sufficient authority that others are able to deal with most situations that might arise.

Only if you're sure it won't wreck your holiday and leave you stewing or seething, phone the office halfway through your break to answer questions or provide advice or direction that will allow co-workers to deal with situations that might otherwise be put on hold until your return.

Schedule your holiday so that your return date doesn't collide with the busiest time of the month. That doesn't mean that you should necessarily plan your holidays so you miss the busy period; but rather that you don't need to return from R & R to be immediately hurled into a wild flurry of activity.

Time your return so that you have a day or two to unpack, sort and settle in at home before you have to head back to the office. If the home side of life is back in some semblance of order (laundry done, bills paid, lawn mowed, fridge stocked), it's easier to dig in on the work side.

Get a head start on your first week back. Sneak into the office over the weekend and sort through the accumulation of notes and papers. Use the solitude to get a handle on the priority tasks that will face you Monday morning.

Don't book a heavy schedule of meetings and commitments for your first day back in the office. You might even ask other staff members to inform callers that you'll be available again and returning calls on a date that is your second day back at work. That will give you some breathing time to get caught up on in-house news and paperwork before you start dealing with the outside world.

Don't go back to work cold turkey! Bring a memento of your vacation to the office – a photo, a seashell, anything that reminds you of what it felt like to be off the treadmill for a few days or weeks.

Build a small reward into your first day back at the grind – lunch with a friend, a browse through a favorite shop or a leisurely walk in the park. Extend that holiday feeling as long as possible!

"It is better to have loafed and lost

than never to have loafed at all."

James Thurber

ALL WORK ... NO PLAY

ENERGY GAIN...ENERGY DRAIN

So ... you've finally found an evening when there's nothing urgent on your schedule. It looks like you've got time to chat with your spouse, play a game with your kids, or dig in to that novel you bought last week.

There's just one problem: you don't have the energy to get off the couch.

Conserving personal energy is just as much of a challenge as managing time. It's a matter of balancing the gains and the drains.

Start by identifying the energy drains in your life.

In a less-than-scientific poll of pooped-out couch potatoes, "negative attitudes and negative people" are the energy drains that repeatedly topped the list. Other responses range from marathon meetings and waiting in line, to paperwork and driving.

Energy drains will be different for everyone. What wears you down may well charge someone else's battery.

Once you know what drains your tank, you've got two choices. You can block as many of those events as possible from your life or link them to activities that give you energy.

For example, if you're stuck having to drive on a lot of long business trips over the next month, you could take a number of linking approaches.

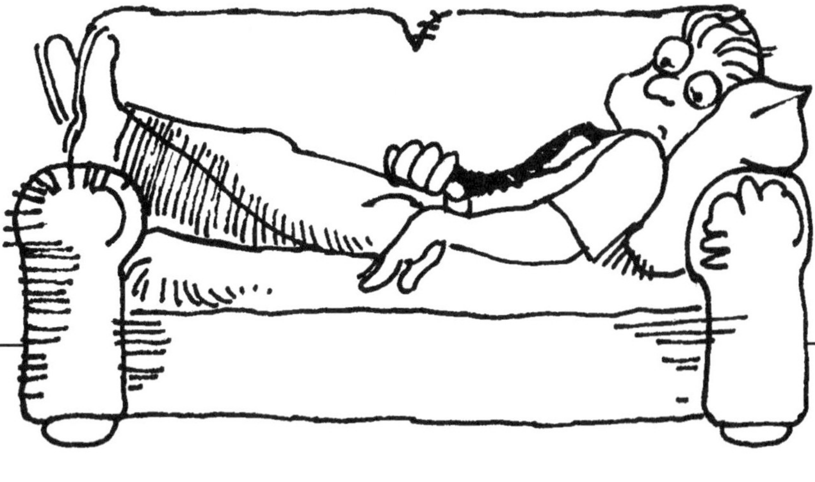

Stock up on audiotapes to play on your car stereo. Comedy performances, books on tape, motivational messages could make the trip more enjoyable. Substitute energizing snacks (fruits, nuts and juices) for chips and sodas. Grab your camera and leave early. Stop to capture the sights along the way. Arrange to take one or two of the trips with someone whose company you enjoy.

Blocking the driving might mean rearranging your itinerary to cut back on the total driving distance, taking a bus, catching a ride with someone else, or arranging a flight for one or more of your trips.

Is a negative co-worker getting you down? Block the energy drain by arranging to spend less time in his or her presence.

Is a long and typically boring staff meeting scheduled for the afternoon? Block the drain by seeing if you can arrange to be present for those parts of the meeting that concern you and excuse yourself for the section that doesn't apply. Link to an energizer by making yourself a soothing pot of tea and taking it into the meeting with you.

Are you deskbound while you pull together this year's annual report or hammer out next year's budget proposal? Link a drain with a gain. Improve the visual appeal of your surroundings. Add fresh flowers or a photo of your favorite holiday get-away for visual refreshment. Arrange to work on the project with an energetic and enthusiastic colleague.

Can't get away from repainting the living room and don't have enough finances to hire someone else to do the job? Invite a buddy to work with you, stock up on your favorite drinks and snacks, and tune in some lively music on the stereo. It's sure to make the job less painful.

"A generation ago most people who finished a day's work needed rest – now they need exercise."

Los Angeles Times Syndicate

ALL WORK... NO PLAY

WORK PLACE TOYS

In medieval times at the King's Court, when tempers flared, tension grew and a beheading seemed certain, courtiers called on the jester for comic relief.

The court clown entertained, soothed and distracted the royalty until cooler heads and reason could prevail.

The days of court jesters and jugglers are long gone. But, thankfully, there are still a lot of fun-loving folks delivering zany punch lines, sharing goofy gadgets and contributing off-the-wall ideas when you least expect it and most need it.

A quick stroll through any toy department yields all kinds of promising diversionary gizmos.

You'll find water pistols artfully disguised as desk staplers and calculators.

There's the ever-traditional paddle board and ball on an elastic string.

Slinkies of all sizes are just right for weighing those difficult decisions and participating in coffee break Slink-A-Thons.

Pull together any set of three (scarves, balls, bean bags, oranges) and teach yourself to juggle. Juggling is a great way to loosen up those rigid neck and shoulders muscles, stretch weary arms and fingers, and relieve eye strain. It's the perfect antidote for all-day drivers and those who are desk or computer bound.

Scout out the Fuzzy Koosh Balls. You won't be able to resist playing with these mopheaded balls that flop in all directions at once. They're an instant adult pacifier and great for juggling, too.

A miniature bubble blower disguised as a pendant turns a fashion accessory into instant entertainment.

Small-scale plastic curling rocks weighted with steel ball bearings slide smoothly down the length of six-foot coffee-room tables, creating a reasonable indoor substitute for a sheet of curling ice. Enjoy your coffee break and a challenge at the same time.

You might have fun with a pop-up digital watch that telescopes in all directions. It's a useful prop for meetings in which you need to send a message to slow-moving chairpersons.

Keep your eyes open and stock up. For less than five dollars you can buy a very serviceable nerf ball, yo-yo or water pistol.

Make a toy basket standard equipment at every work station. Install energizing software that interrupts your work at set intervals to lead you through 60 seconds of stretching exercises or takes you on a brief audio-visual side trip to rest your mind.

You never know when a diversion might be just the thing to restore perspective and energy.

"Enjoy yourself. If you can't enjoy yourself, enjoy somebody else."

Jack Schaefer

ALL WORK... NO PLAY

LET THE FUN BEGIN

"Well, it was exciting to begin with. But the sameness of it all has worn us down. Every year it's the same story. We deal with 'x' in October, 'y' in November, and 'z' in December. We know the rote by heart. We're occasionally thanked for our involvement but it seems like everyone is just going through the motions. No spark!"

If you've worked in the same position for the same organization for a long stretch of time, you might have felt this way yourself. Where did the fun go?

To bring that old sizzle back again, try tossing in a bit more humor, a dash of thoughtfulness and the odd surprise!

If this month's meeting notice looks just like the last one, take a few moments to personalize the reminders. Slip in a cartoon or quote that relates to the main purpose. Include a riddle question or the beginning of a joke. Promise to share the answer or punch line at the start of the next meeting.

Tuck a puzzle piece into each envelope with the agenda. Instruct attendees to bring the pieces to the next meeting and solve it with their colleagues. Offer a prize for the first puzzle solved.

Write a personal note at the bottom of the meeting notice. Add a sprinkle of glitter to each letter. Participants won't soon forget where they were when they opened their envelopes!

Adjust the atmosphere at your next meeting. Make people feel welcome, and let them know you care about their mental and physical well being.

Bring your portable stereo and fill the premeeting air with lively background music. Set a word puzzle on each table as a conversational focus for early arrivals. Hang a couple of inspirational posters.

Add a bouquet of flowers and send them away with someone. Set out a few saucers of jelly beans. Present members with their very own personalized cushions to ease the pain of those long and tedious meetings.

Rethink your meeting tools. Switch to scented markers for your flip chart planning. Why work with stinky alcohol-based markers when you could be scrawling away in grape, cherry or mint? Toss a few neon-colored pens and highlighters on the table to perk up interest in note taking.

Dump the doughnuts and try something new for snacks. Opt for crunchy veggies and fruit or offer a sundae bar with a half-dozen choices for toppings. Bake a batch of fortune cookies with messages tailored to your organization.

Instead of brown bagging your next lunch meeting, try do-it-yourself pizzas or a six-foot submarine sandwich.

Follow the lead of one creative individual who was sure that an upcoming budget debate would be tense. She arrived at the meeting with a gingerbread man for each participant and these instructions: "Sometime during this afternoon's meeting, each one of you is going to feel like biting someone else's head off. Feel free!"

Formalize the fun. Write fun into your job description, and add it to all your program objectives. Elect a Vice-President of Humor or appoint an official jester.

"If ants are such busy workers, how come they find time to go to all those picnics?"
Marie Dressler

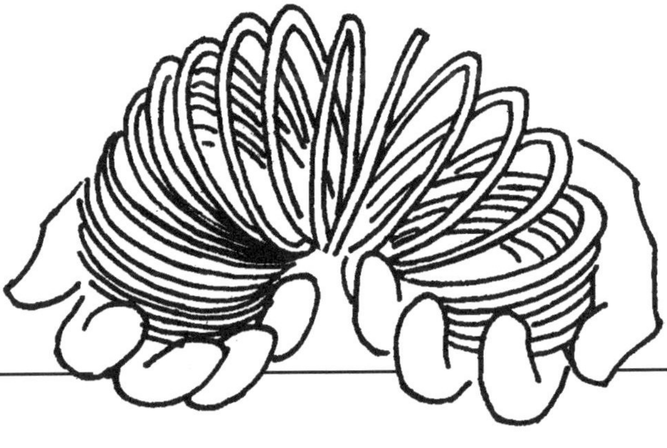

ALL WORK ... NO PLAY

CELEBRATING SUCCESS

Done anything worthy of recognition this week? Did anybody notice?

You can be sure that if you occasionally feel taken for granted at work, so do those around you – employees, colleagues and supervisors.

The fact that someone notices your day-to-day contributions means a lot. In fact, it can make the difference between feeling good about your role at work and asking "Why bother? What's the use?"

When recognizing the actions of others, keep several factors in mind. Not everyone likes to be acknowledged in the same way. Some crave public attention, others shun it. Match your approach to the receiver's preferences. That means you'll need lots of variety in technique.

Repeating the same form of reward loses impact over time, so change your approach regularly.

Mix formal and informal rewards. Five-year certificates and ten-year pins have their place, but it's frequent informal positive feedback that encourages people to keep on going. Be specific about just what it is you are recognizing. "Good job!" or "Way to go!" are short on details.

Get to know people's names and use them often. Add contributors' names to reports and product information. Name an award, a day, a piece of equipment, a product after a key

employee or an employee's child. Use actual employees and clients in advertising photos and annual reports.

Introduce physical tokens of appreciation. Present a pack of lifesavers to someone who helped you out of a jam. Create a travelling basket and fill it with goodies. Award the basket in response to a deserving effort and charge the recipient with replacing the goodies and passing it along to another worthy receiver.

Print thank you's, note cards, or Post-It notes with a message of recognition on the front: Bravo, Pat On The Back, Atta Person, Round of Applause, Great Stuff, etc. Distribute a supply to everyone in the organization. Use them to recognize helpful deeds by writing a few specific comments inside and tucking the cards in places that will surprise the receivers. Send notes to employees' homes so other family members can share the pride.

Think surprise. Fill someone's office with balloons. Dictate jokes and riddles between your letters as you handle your correspondence. Spring for a six-foot submarine sandwich for lunch for the team. Tuck a chocolate bar halfway down a pile of paperwork for a snowed under employee. Hire a professional masseuse to come to the office for a couple of hours to give neck and shoulder massages.

Access to upper management can be a reward in a large organization. Bring senior management down to work the front lines for an afternoon. Involve employees in focus groups to give management feedback on specific business topics. Arrange a coffee break or small group lunch with the C.E.O.

Short stretches of time off can be a much appreciated reward – from an extra break to a long lunch to knocking off two hours early in the afternoon. Cover off the work in the person's absence, so that time off doesn't translate to double time the next day.

Create small celebrations and promote special events to counter the wear and tear of the daily grind. Sponsor a Bad Hat Day or a "Smile-You're-On-Polaroid" Picture Day. Launch a noon Murder Mystery Series or screen comedy videos at lunch.

Remember that recognition is not a magic elixir. All of the encouraging words in the world won't fix serious problems and conflicts that are swept under the carpet and never addressed. Tackle the tough stuff, too!

"Celebrate any progress;

don't wait to get perfect."

Ann McGee Cooper

TIME TRAPS

GOT A MINUTE?

You've just started work on Project X when Joe meanders into your office, plops down in the spare chair, and settles in for a 30-minute chat.

You've just hung up the phone after your third call in as many minutes, and darned if it doesn't ring again.

You've just managed to get your notes and comments together to start on a half hour of dictation, when a sales rep. makes an unexpected visit.

Interruptions are a universal problem. The frustration is extreme. Here's how to keep them to a minimum.

Set aside certain times of your day or week for particular activities. Let others know about your plans.

If you prefer making and receiving calls early in the day, when you leave call back phone messages, tell people that 8:30 a.m. is a good time to reach you.

If you like to spend the first hour after lunch working on priority projects or catching up on correspondence, ask your co-workers to save their questions for later in the afternoon.

If you need two uninterrupted hours on Thursday morning to work on Project X, clear your plan with co-workers.

Schedule regular times to meet with your key people. Spend ten minutes checking signals at the beginning of the week and again once a day. It will shortcircuit interruptions and make it easier for the whole group to schedule work.

Clarify responsibilities and delegate authority to match. If you insist on pulling all the strings, you'll just get tangled up in your own web!

Encourage co-workers and key contacts to keep a running list of questions or information that they want to share with you. That way they can save up a number of nonurgent items and pass them all on at one time – rather than interrupting you for each individual item. Follow the same advice yourself.

Speak up. Tell your drop-in visitor that it isn't a good time for a chat. Make a date for coffee or plan to meet at a more appropriate time.

Cue others through body language. Keep your pen in hand, poised over your paper, as you pausc to tend to the interruption.

Stand up to speak with your visitor rather than inviting that person to settle into a side chair.

If your office desk and chair are situated so that you catch the eye of all passers-by, try giving your desk a quarter turn. Less eye contact means fewer interruptions.

Disappear. If you really need to concentrate on a task without interruptions, arrange to work somewhere else – in a meeting room, an empty office or even at home.

Train and encourage staff to solve problems on their own and reward them when they do.

Pay attention to how you define interruptions and how you react to them. Phones ringing and colleagues and clients with questions are simply part of doing business.

Count your blessings. Breath deep and stay calm. It's far better to be interrupted than to have no business at all!

"The flip side of scheduling private time is scheduling accessible time. Otherwise you risk losing touch ... and damaging relationships."

Stephanie Winston

TIME TRAPS

Someday soon

Unfinished business is a drag! Unstarted business can also weigh you down!

Craft projects started years ago, offhand promises of visits with friends and great ideas for big-selling products all have the same effect. These projects sit in the back of your mind and at the back of your workshop. Occasionally, they trot out reminders: "What's taking so long? What's the matter with you? Are you lazy or something? When are you going to get around to me?"

What blocks action on these commitments to ourselves and others? Lack of time? Lack of energy? Lack of direction? A crippling case of procrastination?

Let's face facts right off the top – there never has been and there never will be enough time or energy to do it all. Tough decisions are required.

Look that list of unfinished and unstarted business straight in the eye. Discard those items that are least important. Toss out the projects that you know in your heart you'll never tackle. Sweep them off your list and out of your mind. Deep-six them forever. Write them on a list and bury it in the backyard if you must.

If you don't think it's important, but your boss or your mate does, find out why. If you still don't agree with the reasoning, negotiate.

Take a good look at the tasks that are left. If some are more important than others, tackle them first. If they all seem to be equally important, start anywhere.

Block out an hour or two each week to devote to these "catch-up, move-ahead" projects. It may not seem like speedy progress, but that's not critical. After all, some of these jobs or ideas have probably been hanging around for years.

Combine the job with something more appealing. Invite a friend or colleague to help, listen to your favorite music while you work, or take the task outside in the sunshine.

Delegate the job to someone else. One person's rotten job is another person's treat.

Be aware that some jobs get worse over time. Remember Mark Twain's advice, "If you've got to swallow a bullfrog, don't look at it too long. If you've got to swallow two bullfrogs, swallow the big one first."

If you don't know where to start on a job, get some advice from those who have tackled similar projects.

Break the job down into small tasks that can be done in 15 or 20 minutes. Do one of these mini tasks. Don't worry about starting in the wrong place; the feedback you receive will point you in the right direction.

Try a leading task. Don't actually start the report or the paint job, just collect all the materials.

Dedicate 30 minutes to the job. Set the timer. When the buzzer rings, you may be far enough into the job that you'll want to continue or you may already be done. If you don't want to keep going, at least you will have made some progress on the task.

Above all, reward yourself! Promise yourself small treats when you finish parts of a job and a bigger treat at the end. You'll deserve them all and they'll keep you going!

"It is well to put off until tomorrow what you ought not to do at all."

Anonymous

TIME TRAPS

Overload Overhaul

Do you keep adding on extra responsibilities and activities without ever dropping anything from the list?

Are you overly optimistic about how quickly you can finish a job – and unrealistic in your estimates?

Have you built such a strong reputation for getting things done that friends and colleagues know they can always count on you to lend a dependable hand with their projects?

Commitment can be a good thing. Too much commitment can be too much of a good thing!

Discovering the reasons why you take on too much can steer you in the direction of a workable antidote. What drives you to say yes one too many times?

Do you have a big heart that feels every need and sees every cause as worthy for your support? Perhaps you worry that if you turn others down it will hurt their feelings.

Are you concerned that if you say no to a task at work, that your name will be added to the dispensable list and you'll be out on the street looking for work?

Possibly you believe your value as a person depends solely on how much you can accomplish.

Avoiding overcommitment requires a good strong sense of who you are and a few tough rounds of priority setting. Knowing what's important helps you weigh the options.

Adjust your expectations to match your time, your energy and your income.

Post some of your invisible time commitments on your calendar so that you have a more realistic picture of how much of your time is available for extra activities.

Choose one or two organizations as the focus of your volunteer effort each year. Play a lesser role in the occasional support of others.

Anticipate the busy periods. Go back and take a look at last year's calendar. See if you can predict those times of year when you are most likely to wade in over your head. Short-circuit the problem by blocking out recharge time and minimizing extra commitments during predictably busy periods.

Don't short yourself on planning time. Check your options. Renegotiate deadlines. Drop or delay a few tasks until later.

Use some of your income to hire help for the tasks you don't like to do, so that you can spend more time on the ones you enjoy.

Slap a sticker on your phone that says, "Think before you say yes!"

Finally, the next time you are in way over your head, take a good close look in the mirror. It's not a pretty sight, is it?

Ask a friend to take your photo. Make a half-dozen prints. Post them everywhere as reminders of the consequences of saying yes once, twice or ten too many times.

"Ask any ten people you meet how they're doing, and nine will respond 'busy'. It's the national disease."

Marshall J. Cook

TIME TRAPS

MAYBE YES! MAYBE NO!

Interested in some great entertainment on a warm summer's night? Pull up a seat at the neighborhood ice cream parlor. Watch the expressions on the faces of the customers as they scan the choices while waiting in line and struggle to make their selections.

What will it be? A banana split, hot fudge brownie or a cone? Will the cone have one, two, or three gravity-defying scoops of ice cream? Will it be pointed, flat bottomed, or a waffle-weave special? What flavor of ice cream goes on top? Rainbow Fudge with Five-Color Sprinkles? Strawberry Bubble Gum Swirl? Rocky Road with Pot Holes & Barricades?

Brain lock is the best description of the state of mind of the average "Ain't it hot? Looking for a treat to cut the heat!" consumer. And a two-dollar ice-cream cone is a minor decision! It's not the end of the world if you discover you don't like Raspberry Rainforest. Next time you can order something else.

But brain lock isn't limited to the ice-cream counter; and many decisions have tougher consequences and longer lasting side effects.

When you tackle the tougher problems, these approaches may help you wade through the swamp of indecision.

Revisit your original objective. What were you trying to accomplish in the first place?

Summarize what you know already about the problem or opportunity. Take a moment to note the pros and cons of solutions you have identified so far. Rank the pros and cons by relative importance and weigh the risks involved in each approach.

Ask yourself what extra information might be useful in making your decision and how you might go about collecting it. Where is the information located? Who could help you with the search?

Seek out others who have faced similar questions and see what wisdom they have to share.

Contrast the merits and consequences of waiting for further information versus acting on what you know so far. A speedier decision could move things forward and give you more time to correct unexpected problems that arise.

Assess the importance of the decision. Allow an appropriate amount of time for making it. Practice making quick decisions on insignificant issues. Ice cream and doughnut selections are 30 second – not 30 minute – choices.

Narrow the field by eliminating those options that are definitely out of the running so you are dealing with fewer possibilities.

Recognize when you have enough information or when you aren't going to get any more or better information even if you wait any longer. Then go ahead and decide.

Once you've made a decision, move on. Don't torture yourself or waste time by continuing to check other options, prices and possibilities.

If it's the indecisive nature of your boss or spouse or that's holding up progress, do whatever you can to encourage action. Ask questions. Provide information. Summarize. Test proposals and options.

"Time, like a snowflake, disappears while we're trying to decide what to do with it."

St. Louis Bugle

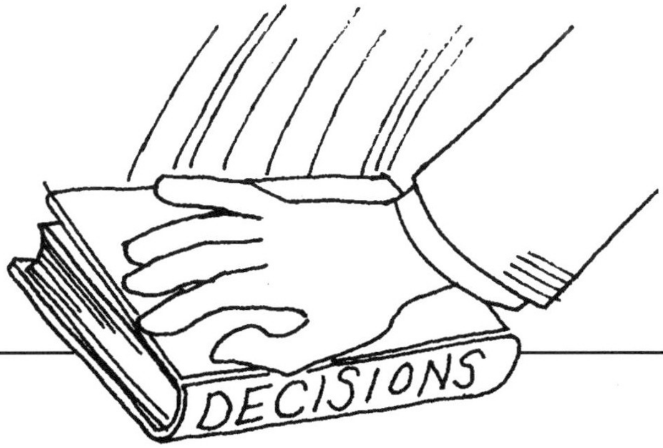

TIME TRAPS

BACKLOGS

Three hundred years ago, a backlog was a large log at the rear of a fire that might be big enough to smolder for days. The fact that a backlog could last for a very long time made it even more valuable. It was an important asset – a reserve or a source of great potential – like a packet of seeds or a jar of sourdough starter.

A 1932 article in the Baltimore Sun refers to a backlog as an arrears of unfulfilled orders. That's still an accumulation of great value – sales in waiting, as it were.

Today's backlogs are more often viewed as a burden than a resource – the cause of much wailing and gnashing of teeth. "How did we get so far behind? How will we ever get through it all?"

Whether it's invoicing, correspondence, filing or manufacturing on the workfront – or laundry, clean-up or bill paying on the homefront – there are several ways to approach backlogs so they can be handled in an effective manner.

Take stock of the extent of the problem. Don't overreact and let yourself get overwhelmed. Take real measurements. List the tasks that need to be handled and guesstimate the time and resources involved.

Set priorities in the areas that are creating the biggest headache or have the potential of causing the greatest harm or loss. Or, alternately, choose the task that will make the largest dent in the backlog and inspire you to further action. Assign your resources to those areas first.

Consider drastic measures. Weigh the potential risks of discarding some of the items that are part of the backlog. What would be the impact of setting the entire backlog aside and simply starting in from where you are now?

Sort jobs and group materials, so those tasks that are similar in approach or those which use the same kind of equipment can be handled at the same time.

Schedule a blitz effort. Pull together a backlog attack team to give it all they've got for a weekend or for a few hours a day in the coming week.

Look for business and personal services that specialize in your kind of problem.

Farm out either the ongoing regular tasks or the backlog itself – for short periods of time or indefinitely. Invite estimates from other manufacturers or service suppliers on the cost of outside help.

Think big-time solutions for big-time backlogs. If the situation were 2 or 3 times its current size, how would you handle it? Would it pay to take that same approach right now and get the problem out of the way quickly?

Ask yourself what you might be saying that is compounding the pressure. Does this really have to be done by the end of the week or is there some flexibility in the outside or self-imposed deadline?

Don't let a backlog send you into a tailspin and a slow burn. Look it squarely in the eye and fire up your resources.

"This constant, unproductive preoccupation with all the things we have to do is the single largest consumer of time and energy."

Kerry Gleeson

STREAMLINING OPTIONS

CLUES AND CUES

Increased productivity – getting more done in less time with fewer people – has become a nationwide preoccupation. Valued employees are those who pinpoint streamlining opportunities and make them work.

Lightening the burden of a workload that never ends and slicing away workplace stresses are great incentives for sliding "common practice" under the microscope.

These suggestions will help you create a leaner, meaner workplace – one that could just be a tad more humane.

Pay close attention to tasks that are delegated to you or that you assign to others over the next month or quarter. Keep a journal of your observations and questions.

Tune in to your frustrated self-talk: "Why am I doing this? Nobody looks at this!" Follow through on those internal comments and ask around. What is the reason for doing the job in question? Who actually does look at the information that you are pulling together and in what detail?

Listen to the comments and frustrations of colleagues with a questioning attitude as well as a sympathetic ear and shoulder. Maybe their complaint contains the seed of a streamlining opportunity.

Invite new employees to question activities that seem unnecessary or procedures that seem more complicated than necessary. Sometimes a fresh pair of eyes will see clearly what more experienced ones take for granted.

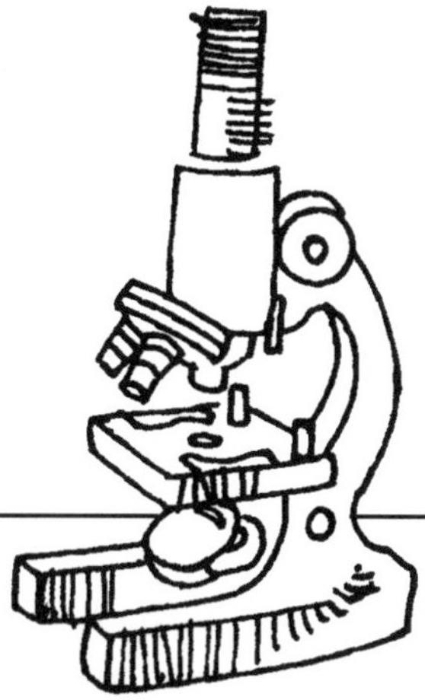

Carry out a paper and process audit. Trace the routes for certain reports, forms and decisions. Ask yourself: How often is this document generated? How long does it take to put it together? Is this information later revised and turned out in a different form? Who sees it, reads it or approves it? Why do we create it? How is it useful to the organization? Are there wasted steps in its creation or approval? Which of these steps do our customers really care about? Collect specific data – not just general impressions – and write it down.

Take note of any duplication of efforts – rewriting of reports for the next level of management, duplicate filing of the same information, generation of unnecessary multiple copies, separate systems tracking the same information, old systems maintained alongside new systems, well past a normal period of caution.

Pull out those equipment manuals – the ones that came with the new system that no one had time to read. Scan the table of contents and index looking for shortcuts that no one is using.

Reflect on the adjustments that are made to work loads and work patterns when staff members take vacations. Could some of the approaches used during holiday periods (when you are short staffed) be extended through the entire year?

Quiz employees in other branch offices of your organization about their streamlining efforts. What have they stopped doing recently and with what results?

Swap streamlining ideas and approaches with others in totally unrelated businesses. You never know when an idea from another field can be adapted to yours.

Enjoy the fruits of your streamlining labors. Take a real coffee break. Enjoy a work-free weekend. Trade jokes with someone at the office. Breathe!

"Our life is frittered away by detail, simplify! Simplify! Simplify!"

Henry David Thoreau

STREAMLINING OPTIONS

DOWNSIZING DILEMMAS

"Nine branches are closing and 150 people are being laid off in an effort to improve the competitive advantage of the organization."

"Twenty positions are being eliminated from our department, but service to the public will not be affected."

The daily news is full of reports about downsizing. Rest assured that downsizing does not involve sorting goose feathers, nor does it have anything to do with measuring the speed of escalators.

Downsizing is not about washing woolens in hot water and tossing them into a hot dryer. Although folks who have been through the downsizing operation, say that feelings of having been "hung out to dry" and "put through the wringer" do apply.

Downsizing is a strategy for cutting costs, balancing budgets and staying in business. It usually means reducing the size of the work force – laying people off or eliminating positions vacated through retirement or resignation.

The net result of downsizing is that those employees and supervisors who have not been cut inherit jobs that have been resized – read expanded. It's a rare organization that downsizes the workload when it downsizes the work force.

Most people can carry extra responsibilities for limited periods of time. It's when today's "limited period of time" starts to

become tomorrow's "everyday expectation" that employees begin to wear out.

Sizing workloads by piling on the responsibilities until colleagues or employees begin to falter, cry uncle, or excuse themselves on extended stress or sick leave is a dangerous practice.

There is an alternative. It begins with developing a consistently high level of time-management skills – clarifying purposes, setting goals, choosing priorities, scheduling and delegating effectively. It continues with open discussion and negotiation – at every level – about new assignments and workload design.

When employees and managers have clear long-term goals, up-to-date priorities, specific plans for projects, and scheduled target dates, they have a more accurate picture of how much of their time is currently committed. They are in a much better position to take a realistic look at new demands on their time.

To maintain healthy workers and a healthy work place, when extra assignments arise, review these four points: the size of the task, the detail in which it needs to be carried out, extra resources available to bring it off, and the deadline for completion.

What is involved in the task? How long will it take? How does its importance stack up in relation to previously agreed upon priorities?

In what detail does the task need to be carried out? Are ball-park estimates sufficient or will detailed research be required? In light of the rest of the workload, are there some standards that can be reduced in status from "perfection required" to "good enough will be fine".

Is it possible to contract out parts of this or another task. Can extra hands be hired on a temporary basis? Is overtime an acceptable alternative?

What degree of flexibility is there in the stated deadline? Can the job be split into several pieces, delivering the first portion by the original deadline with other parts following at later dates? Can deadlines be renegotiated on other projects to accommodate this new priority?

These approaches are not "them versus us" or "your-side/our-side" knock-down labor negotiations. They are open and frank discussions about what's reasonably possible for both long-term employee health and organizational success.

STREAMLINING OPTIONS

ONE-PERSON BIZ...TWO-PERSON LOAD

There are advantages to operating a one-person business. Meetings are short. Office politics don't waste much time. Clearing holiday schedules is straight forward. Internal communication is fast. Drawing an organizational chart is a snap.

Still, there are complications. Three clients need you at the same time. Your family planned a night at the movies that conflicts with your plans for a night at the ledgers. You have ten tasks that could be delegated but in scanning your small one-person office, you don't see another soul prepared to take on the job.

Short of cloning yourself, or becoming a full- or part-time employer, you might consider other options.

Track your administrative time so you know where your time goes now. How many hours a month does it take to run errands, stock supplies, update the books? Maybe you could afford to delegate or contract one or more of these responsibilities; but first, you need to know how much time is involved.

Speak with current service providers to see how they could help you streamline your work. Secretarial services will do more than type letters. They'll also bind reports, stuff mailings and run your envelopes through a postage meter.

Familiarize yourself with all the time and money-saving options your suppliers offer. Ask about free delivery, extended hours, toll-free or fax order services. Have you been standing at a self-serve copier when your local print shop will handle the copying for you at self-serve prices?

If you've been paying cash each time you use the services of another business, open an account. Write one cheque in response to a monthly invoice instead of handling several cash transactions each month.

Check out the services provided by your bank or credit union. Have you been standing in long line-ups at the cash counter, when you could have speedier access to side-counter service for business transactions?

Consider using a moderately priced courier service to run your business errands and free up time for other tasks.

Multiply your efforts. Track your most frequent types of inquiries and pull together a standard information package that can be popped in the mail in response.

Make your current technology work for you. Learn to use all the features on your telephone. Get yourself up to speed on the software that's already on your computer.

Rethink how you use the technology that's right at hand. When a potential client calls, enter the name and address right into the database on your computer instead of scrawling it on a piece of paper. If you've streamlined the handling of correspondence in your business, as soon as the call is over, you will be ready to pop out a form letter response and a mailing label with very little extra effort.

Invest in a fax machine or subscribe to an electronic mail service. Cut down on the time spent in line-ups at the post office. Add a fax modem to your computer so you don't need to print paper to send and receive information.

If you are wasting time searching for the nearest pay phone, maybe a cellular phone should be moved up a notch on your acquisition wish list.

Those who have a sound understanding of their manual accounting system might consider moving to a computerized system. Good-bye paper tapes! Hello instant totals!

"Entrepreneurs work 12 hours a day for themselves so they won't have to work 8 hours a day for someone else!"

Source Unknown

MANY HANDS - LIGHT WORK

DELEGATION THAT WORKS

Workplace delegation is a two-way street. If your delegation style causes problems down the line, you're likely to find those problems headed right back at you!

There are six steps for successfully getting things done with and through other people.

Keep these six steps in mind. Tack them on the corner of your bulletin board, or discuss them with co-workers.

Whenever someone delegates a major task to you, mentally run through the six-step checklist. If one or more points have been omitted, ask for the information.

Above all, keep the communication flowing both ways. It's the "not-so-secret" basic ingredient for effective delegation.

Step One: Establish the need for the task. This is the delegation acid test. If you can't come up with a sound reason for why a job needs to be done, maybe it doesn't!

Delegation is the wrong way to dispose of the unnecessary. If it's within your power, drop the task altogether. If that decision is beyond your authority, negotiate its demise.

Step Two: Describe the task in detail. Too many tasks are delegated by the "Dump and Run" delivery system. The job is dumped in someone else's lap as the delegator runs out the door – no instructions, no support, no deadlines! This technique does nothing to improve working relationships.

Be sure to provide full details if you are inexperienced at delegation or you are delegating a task to an inexperienced colleague, if you are delegating tasks to a new co-worker, or if the task is complicated.

Not all instructions need to be written out in longhand. You can describe the task in person. You can design a simple check sheet to attach to paperwork and simply fill in the blanks. Or, if your writing is poor or the message is lengthy, you can dictate simple instructions on a cassette recorder.

Step Three: Set follow-up deadlines. Never delegate or accept a task with an A.S.A.P deadline. "As Soon As Possible" could mean "before noon", "by Friday", or "sometime next summer when you have nothing else to do".

Attach realistic target dates to all delegated tasks. Noting specific deadlines on projects helps others organize their workloads and avoids misunderstandings. If the deadline is flexible, say so. If it turns out to be unrealistic, negotiate.

Step Four: Confirm understanding. Ask the delegatee to repeat the instructions for you, or to review the first couple of steps in tackling the assignment. You'll have a better idea of how much of the task is understood and where you'll need to watch for problems.

Step Five: Make support available. Some projects require special resources (money, facilities, equipment, access to information, extra help). Anticipate the needs; and pave the way for the use of these resources.

Step Six: Follow up as planned. Note intermediate deadlines on your calendar. Ask for progress reports, and initiate follow-up meetings.

"Plans get you into things but you've got to work your way out."
Will Rogers

MANY HANDS - LIGHT WORK

TRACKING DELEGATION

Although delegation is very much a matter of trust; successful delegation depends on timely and appropriate follow-up.

If you've forgotten to whom you delegated a job, or when you were expecting it to be done, it's tough to check on progress.

Writing things down will help. Let those to whom you delegate know that you are recording due dates and develop a system that helps you follow up as needed. It's a habit that prompts timely activity on the part of others.

Choose one system for tracking delegated tasks, and use it with regularity.

You can track delegated tasks by noting follow up actions on the specific dated page of your calendar. Designate one area of your calendar page for follow-up activities to help you pinpoint them more quickly.

If you maintain a "tickler" or "bring-forward" file, simply toss a note in the file for the appropriate follow-up day.

Creating separate project or delegation sections in your planner can also be effective.

When co-ordinating a major project, set up a record sheet for delegated tasks and intermediate deadline dates as part of the project plan.

Those who supervise a number of different people, may set up a planning notebook section that includes a delegation record sheet for each individual. Note each task as it is delegated and record the date assigned and date due. Review these pages in your planner every day or two.

A delegation record for each employee will also help you track how many and what types of tasks you are delegating to each person. This can help balance assignments and workloads.

Planning and calendar software can help you track assigned jobs. Note due dates and set computer alarms to bring tasks to your attention on appropriate days at appropriate times.

Some software packages will manage recurring tasks for you. If you need to check with your secretary the day before each regular monthly staff meeting to see that all the necessary arrangements have been made, simply enter this activity as a recurring task to appear the day prior to the monthly meeting date.

You want to give those you work with the best possible chance to succeed at delegated tasks. When appropriate, set your reminders so that you can check in to see how the task is coming along early on the due date or a day or two before the actual due date.

This lets the person ask for advice or information that will help complete the project on time. In the case of a task that has been overlooked, your advance checking helps the delegatee save face ("Oh, yes, it's coming along just fine!") and still get the job done on time. That is, after all, what you are trying to accomplish in the first place.

"A good delegator is like a catalyst: he or she causes something to happen without being used up in the process. If you don't delegate, or if you delegate ineffectively, you will get used up."

Source Unknown

MANY HANDS-LIGHT WORK

JUNIOR BUSINESS PARTNERS

A business operating from home has a direct impact on the family. It eats up space, time and attention. It also offers rewards: revenue, challenge and a chance to see other family members in a different light.

Entrepreneurs often choose to be homebased in an attempt to balance work and family interests. And, although children can make it difficult to concentrate on business, they can also be valuable contributors.

Family labor is not only helpful to the business owner who is often stretched to the limit; it also introduces youngsters to the world of entrepreneurship.

To enlist your family members in your business efforts, begin by listing activities with which you could use some help: production, packaging, purchasing, delivery, advertising, bookkeeping, sales, computing or maintenance.

Be on the lookout for jobs to delegate. Keep a running list of "Junior Tasks".

Ask other business people how they involve their youngsters. Ask your own kids how they would like to be involved.

Some tasks are great for those with willing hearts but short attention spans. Cleaning up around the production area, emptying the garbage, stuffing and licking envelopes, collating handouts or delivering flyers fall into this category.

Other jobs are great for reinforcing basic skills. Counting inventory and alphabetically filing papers or business cards are examples.

Be on the lookout for opportunities to call on special skills. Perhaps your talented artist could create a drawing for your advertising. The computer whiz could prepare form letters and run mailing labels. If you discover both skills in one child, invest in a computer drawing program.

What and how much you delegate will depend on the age, interests and maturity of the youngsters. You'll also need to consider how much time they are able to contribute.

It's only fair to compensate the junior members of your business team for their efforts. You may choose to pay cash or reward them with bonus activities (e.g., two hours of stuffing envelopes will get you a free movie pass!)

For cash payment to youngsters to be allowed as a legitimate business expense, payment must be reasonably in line with the amount and type of services performed. Educate yourself about tax rules for payment of casual labor.

If you want to really make your youngsters feel like an important part of your business, give your junior workers appropriate job titles (Maintenance Coordinator, File Clerk, Art Director, Circulation Supervisor, Manager of Hugs & Humor Services).

Print up a supply of business cards with their names on the front. They're great for dropping into the "free lunch draws" at restaurants around town and for impressing friends and family.

Draw up an employment contract. Negotiate the tasks and the timing. Be flexible – just like you would with any other employee – but be clear about performance expectations.

Above all, avoid the slave and master approach to employee relations. "I'll crack the whip, you'll jump to attention." That approach doesn't do much to promote employee motivation in the general work world. It's even less effective when involving family members in the business!

"I use not only the brains I have, but all that I can borrow."

Woodrow Wilson

MANY HANDS - LIGHT WORK

EFFECTIVE COMMITTEES

Is the term, "effective committee", really an oxymoron? You know – an unlikely possibility – like "military intelligence" or "delicious porridge"?

There's no doubt committees get bad press. Victor Riesel described a committee as, "a group of the unfit, appointed by the unwilling to do the unnecessary." A cynical view, to be sure!

With all the scorn heaped on committees, you might wonder why they continue to exist. The answer is clear. Despite their shortcomings, committees can and do work.

Organizations greatly multiply their achievements by effectively delegating work to subgroups. Progress through committees is possible.

Choose the right type of committee for the job.

Standing committees (like Finance, Public Relations and Executive Committees) have an ongoing function. Committee membership is often specified by position in the organization (e.g., the Vice-President may automatically be a member of the Finance Committee).

Ad hoc committees are formed to carry out specific tasks (e.g., to develop a grant application or to organize a special event). Ad hoc committees have a limited life. Their members are named because of an interest in the task or because of the special skills or knowledge they bring to the group.

Once you've chosen a committee style that fits the task, give your committee the best start possible. Clarify its purpose, authority, resources, deadlines and communication requirements.

Outline the exact nature of the job. Be specific so that the committee can dig right into the task and so that members will know when their goals have been met. Rank the assignments in order of importance. Describe how these activities fit into the "big picture" or overall goals of the organization. Include a termination clause for ad hoc committees (i.e., The committee will disband by a certain date or on the completion of a particular task).

Indicate how freely the committee can act on its decisions. Must the group's plan first be approved by the executive, or does the committee have free reign to act independently in performing all or part of the task?

Set out available resources. What is the budget for this activity? What other resources (e.g., staff members, computing time) are available? How can the group access these resources?

Map out intermediate milestones and final deadlines. Explain how target dates tie into other activities of the organization.

Clearly specify how often and to whom the committee is expected to communicate its progress and whether reports should be written or verbal.

Consider the ideal size of the group and the kind of expertise or representation that is needed to make the group tick. Keep committees as small as possible with wide enough representation to act with confidence.

Brief all committee members on the organization's expectations. Invite questions to be certain that all aspects of the assignment are clear.

Charge one individual in the group with the responsibility of calling the first meeting and getting things underway.

"The middle of every successful project looks like a disaster."

Rosabeth Moss Cantor

LIFELONG LEARNING

MAKING THE MOST OF TRAINING

Training costs and training pays. It consumes time and money. It improves skill and confidence. Use these suggestions to make the most of your own training experiences.

Choose the topic and type of event that stretches your mind. If you are entirely comfortable at a training event, and can predict what the presenter will say next, then you're in the wrong session.

Scan seminar advertisements for clues to the level of difficulty. Key words like "simple, basic, introductory, beginning" all signal that the material is geared to novices.

If you've attended several seminars on the same topic and are still having trouble applying the theory, you may not benefit from a lecture-style program. Ask about planned-teaching approaches. Ideas transfer more easily from the classroom to the workplace when hands-on skill practices are included.

If you have very precise needs or specific questions about a topic, consider one-on-one consulting help.

Set your own learning goals. Pinpoint the ideas or help that you hope this session will provide.

On training day, let office mates know that you will be in a training session. Ask not to be interrupted except in case of emergencies. (Define emergencies!)

Sit up front where you can see what's going on and be a part of the action. If several people from your organization are attending, split up. Use the opportunity to make new contacts and listen to fresh ideas.

For comfort, dress in layers that can be added or discarded. Hotels and training facilities are notorious for their Arctic-Sahara climates.

Take all the necessary materials to the session, including a pen and paper. Seem obvious? Check out how many people arrive without!

Take notes, even if a handout is provided. Your own notes will help you recall important points. If the resource person allows, you could record the presentation for later reference.

Set up an "Action Sheet" and keep it in front of you throughout the session. When you discover an idea you want to use right away, note it down.

Be an active participant in your own learning. Offer suggestions. Ask questions. Volunteer for a role play.

If an assigned individual exercise seems totally useless, do something else with your time: outline a project; set some goals; draft a letter; play with a problem.

Use session breaks to: take a few notes on how to apply the information to your own situation; network and make contacts; relax and refresh yourself. Avoid calling back to the office. It will just split your concentration.

When you return to the office, post your Action Reminder notes on your bulletin board or add them to your Master List. This will jump start the skill transfer from class to real life.

Summarize the key points of the session for a colleague, your manager or an employee. Sharing with others helps crystallize the information.

Build "on-the-job" support for any changes you hope to make. Enlist the help of a peer or a manager as a coach. Ask your coach to: support your actions; hold you accountable for following through on your plans for change; celebrate your progress.

Look for opportunities to practise new skills and implement new ideas as soon after the session as possible.

"To teach is to learn twice."

Japanese Proverb

LIFELONG LEARNING

RETAINING RETRAINING

You'll find them lounging on office book shelves, loitering in mountainous reading piles, and lurking in the darkest recesses of your filing cabinet drawers.

These parchment remains of conferences and seminars take many forms. Some have been dutifully filed and organized. Others have been beautifully bound and magnificently processed.

Most of them are still crammed into the canvas conference tote bag or vinyl folder from the event that gave them birth. All were compiled in the spirit of good intentions.

From hastily scratched notes to elaborate handouts, they are telling records of ideas that came "that close" to being put into action.

This transfer of great ideas and insights into workplace action is a huge challenge. These suggestions will improve the likelihood of action and cut down on the number of buried remains from seminars past.

As you begin your next training experience, summarize the problems or issues that led you to this particular program. What answers are you hoping to find? What information are you hoping to glean from the session?

Learn to think like a miner. If you have some idea of what you're looking for, you're more likely to recognize it when it shows up.

As you make your way through the material, jot down key ideas that you think will help solve those problems. Develop a one-page summary sheet of learning nuggets.

Comprehensive notes make great reference materials, but a short list of critical insights is worth its weight in gold. Post your nuggets on your bulletin board.

Compile your nugget sheets in one binder to create an ongoing summary of key ideas – old learnings to remember and new learnings to incorporate.

Set your binder by the phone where you can review highlights of recent programs while you're waiting on hold. Or carry your keepers in your car where you can thumb through the collection between appointments.

You might even create your own audio tape featuring the top-ten learning points from each program. Record some reminders and a few new insights. Fill the space between each set of ideas with a musical interlude that encourages you to reflect on how and whether you are actually using the information.

Refreshing yourself in any one of these ways will help keep those important learnings in the forefront of your mind throughout your working week. It may also cut down on the guilt experienced when you next uncover the archaeological remains of seminars past.

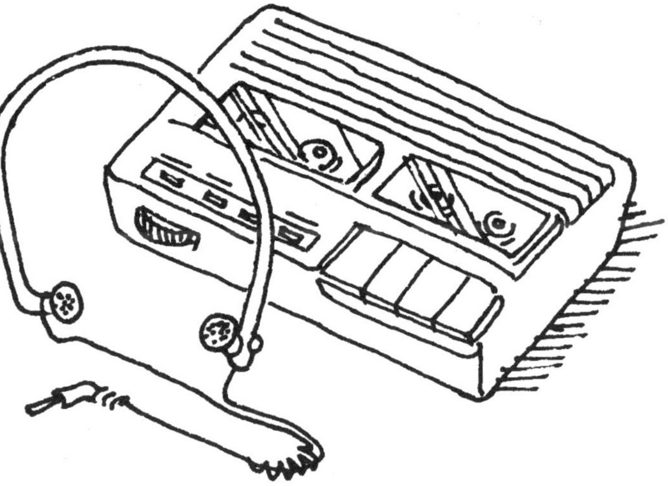

"There are two kinds of knowledge: knowing something, and knowing who knows it."
Samuel Johnson

LIFELONG LEARNING

NIGHT SCHOOL KNOW-HOW

Admiration! That's what so many of the adults who are hitting the books in their "spare" time deserve. Upgrading, retraining and certification is the name of the game.

It's not easy to juggle paid work, family responsibilities and volunteer commitments. Add to those demands an extra night class or correspondence program, and you multiply the challenges. Here's how some folks cope.

Next to financing, scheduling is the most common stumbling block. Clearing the decks of extra responsibilities at work and easing back on volunteer hours is often required.

Renegotiating household tasks may also be in order. Simplifying meals (more take out, leftovers, or soup and sandwich specials) make the mad dash to an evening class possible.

Scheduling homework and study time can be even tougher. Class hours may be respected, but when it's just mom with the books at the kitchen table, she may be considered fair game for interruptions.

Early birds try to use those early morning hours to academic advantage. Night owls wait until the rest of the family has gone to bed before setting up study hall.

A separate study area (a desk in the bedroom or spare room) can make it easier to concentrate while others are up and around. Some students put in the extra hours away from home – at the library or elsewhere. They may use their desks or boardrooms in their workplaces or spare office space at a spouse's place of business. These locations often provide off-hours access to computer equipment for preparing assignments.

It's possible to make effective use of other bits and pieces of time by playing a walkman or micro cassette recorder during commuting or exercise time to study facts and figures that need to be memorized. Devoting earned days off to extra study and exam preparation helps ease the pressure.

Some adult students team up with other learners to divide research responsibilities and prepare mini-tutorials for each other. A few enterprising souls hire fellow students or family members to search out library reference materials and articles for review.

Breaking large assignments down into smaller pieces, setting intermediate deadlines for the completion of various stages, tracking project due dates, and coordinating the required clerical support are critical elements in bringing projects in on time.

Savvy learners make class case studies serve double duty by using real-life workplace examples. They create opportunities to weave together work activities and class projects.

When class materials and papers get out of hand, setting up an indexed binder can make the flurry of paperwork more manageable. Some of these categories will do the trick: class contact lists, notes, reading lists, handouts, assignments, labs, etc.

Successful adult learners take personal responsibility for their success. They let instructors know what they need and expect by way of lead time on assignments, in-class review, supplementary resource materials, extra tutoring and accessibility for extra help.

And finally, those learners who stay motivated over the long haul remember to reward their own efforts. They plan appropriate treats and celebrations after each exam, at the conclusion of major papers and when they get their final marks.

Dancing in the streets is not excessive! There's no doubt they've earned a party!

BOOKS . . . BOOKS . . . AND . . . MORE . . . BOOKS

For more information and inspiration check out the following recommended references. The brief notes on each reference will help you pick a resource that will fit your needs.

Among the listings, you'll find books that:

— *offer suggestions on specific workplace problem areas;*
— *deal with organizing basics, styles and general principles; and*
— *focus on the big picture – clarifying purpose and values.*

Alesandrini, Kathryn, **Survive Information Overload**, Business One Irwin, 1992. *Techniques for dealing with the unending sources of information in our work and personal lives.*

Aslett, Don, **The Office Clutter Cure**, Marsh Creek Press, 1994. *How to minimize office clutter with special sections on common areas and mental clutter.*

Bittel, Lester, **Right On Time**, McGraw Hill, 1991. *An analytical look at time and project management.*

Bliss, Edwin C., **Getting Things Done**, Bantam Books, 1976. *An alphabetic reference to time management problems and solutions.*

Bliss, Edwin, **Doing It Now**, Bantam Books, 1983. *A 12-step program for curing procrastination and achieving goals.*

Booher, Dianna, **Clean Up Your Act!**, Warner Books, 1992. *Great ideas for simplifying written communication.*

Burka, Jane & Yuen, Lenora, **Procrastination**, Addison Wesley Publishing Company, 1983. *A probing exploration of the fears and roots of procrastination and what to do about it.*

Caddylak, **The Complete Portfolio of Time Management Forms**, Caddylak Publishing, 1984. *Almost 200 calendar and planning forms of all shapes, sizes and layouts.*

Cook, Marshall, **Slow Down & Get More Done**, Betterway Books, 1993. *Taking responsibility for setting your own pace, building in time for relaxation and renewal.*

Cooper, Ken, **Always Bear Left**, Dell Publishing Co. Inc., 1982. *Shortcuts and quick ways to get things done.*

Covey, Stephen with Merrill, Roger and Rebecca, **First Things First**, Simon & Schuster, 1994. *Aligning your use of time and energy with your highest purpose and values.*

Covey, Stephen R., **The Seven Habits of Highly Effective People**, Simon & Schuster, 1989. *A principle and value centerd examination of how we spend our lives. Insightful and challenging.*

Culp, Stephanie, **Conquering The Paper Pile-Up**, Writer's Digest Books, 1990. *Paper handling equipment and systems for home and office.*

Culp, Stephanie, **Streamlining Your Life**, Writer's Digest Books, 1991. *A five-point plan for uncomplicated living.*

Culp, Stephanie, **You Can Find More Time For Yourself Every Day**. Betterway Books, 1994. *Changing the way you think about time and using it in the most satisfactory ways.*

Davidson, Jeff, **Breathing Space**, MasterMedia Ltd., 1991. *Why the pace of life has become so hectic and what to do about it.*

Declan Treacy, **Clean Your Desk**, Business Books Limited, 1991. *A direct attack on paper work and desktop clutter.*

Eyre, Linda and Richard, **Lifebalance**, Ballantine Books, 1987. *Great book focusing on balancing priorities, attitudes and goals.*

Fanning, Tony and Robbie, **Get It All Done & Still Be Human**, Kali House, 1990. *Very well written. Many useful techniques including patterning model.*

Gleeson, Kerry, **The Personal Efficiency Program,** John Wiley and Sons, 1994. *Useful section on organizing electronic files and information.*

Griessman, Eugene, **Time Tactics of Very Successful People**, McGraw Hill, 1994. *Experiences of successful people organized into principles for productive action.*

Hemphill, Barbara, **Taming The Paper Tiger**, Kiplinger, 1992. *Paper handling techniques for work and home.*

Kanarek, Lisa, **Organizing Your Home Office For Success**, Plume Books, 1993. *A comprehensive reference to furnishing, equipping, and arranging your home office.*

Kelly, Al, **How To Make Your Life Easier At Work**, Avon Books, 1988. *Managing your workday for high efficiency and low stress.*

Keyes, Ralph, **Timelock**, Harper Collins, 1991. *Finding ways to decelerate time-pressured schedules.*

Klein, Ruth, **Where Did The Time Go?** Prima Publishing, 1993. *A working woman's guide to creative time management at work and home.*

Kofodimos, Joan, **Balancing Act**, Jossey Bass, 1993. *How managers can integrate successful careers and fulfilling personal lives.*

Lakein, Alan, **How to Get Control of Your Time and Your Life**, The New American Library Inc., 1974. *A pioneer and early classic in time management.*

LeBoeuf, Michael, **Working Smart**, Warner Books, 1979. *Focuses on bringing the greatest return from your investment of time and energy. Good chapter on "New Attitudes for Effectiveness".*

Lehmkuhl, Dorothy & Cotter Lamping, Dolores, **Organizing For The Creative Person**, Crown Trade Paperbacks, 1993. *How left- or right-brain dominance influences your organizing style and preferences.*

Mackenzie, R. Alec, **The Time Trap**, Amacom, 1990. *An updated version of an early classic in time management.*

Mallinger, Allan & De Wyze, Jeannette, **Too Perfect**, Clarkson Potter Publishers, 1992. *Specially directed to those obsessed with perfection and control.*

Mayer, Jeffrey, **If You Haven't Got The Time To Do It Right, When Will You Find The Time To Do It Over?**, Simon and Schuster, 1990. *Sections on making your desk and your day work for you.*

Mayer, Jeffrey, **Time Management For Dummies**, IDG Books, 1995. *Large sections on communications and computing as a tool for greater productivity.*

Mayer, Jeffrey, **Time Management Survival Guide For Dummies**, IDG Books, 1995. *Special sections covering working in your home office and on the road.*

McGee-Cooper, Ann, **Time Management for Unmanageable People**, Bantam Books, 1994. *Workable ideas for the creative, inspired and hopelessly disorganized.*

McGee-Cooper, Ann, **You Don't Have To Go Home From Work Exhausted**, Bowen and Rogers, 1990. *Wonderful read and exciting presentation! How to add energy enhancers and rejuvenators to every day of your life.*

O'Neil, John R., **The Paradox of Success — When Winning At Work Means Losing At Life**, Putnam, 1993. *Techniques and challenges for renewing ourselves in both our professional and personal lives.*

Pollar, Odette, **Organizing Your Workspace**, Crisp Publications, 1992. *Workspace organizing basics presented in a workbook format.*

Robinson, Dr. Bryan, **Overdoing It — How To Slow Down And Take Care Of Yourself**, Health Communications, Inc., 1992. *A 12-step recovery approach to overcommitment and overdoing.*

Schlenger, Sunny, and Roesch, Roberta, **How to be Organized In Spite of Yourself**, Penguin Books, 1989. *Specific solutions for problems associated with each of ten different organizational styles.*

Sher, Barbara, **I Could Do Anything If I Only Knew What It Was**, Delacorte Press, 1994. *Tools and exercises for clarifying values, life purpose and career direction.*

Silver, Susan, **Organized To Be The Best!**, Adams-Hall Publishing, 1989. *Great resource for work-place organization.*

Simon, Dr. Sidney, **In Search Of Values**, Warner Books, 1993. *31 strategies for finding out what really matters most to you.*

Smith, Hyrum W., **The 10 Natural Laws of Successful Time & Life Management**, Warner Books, 1994. *Strategies for increased productivity and inner peace.*

Swenson, Richard A., **Margin, How To Create The Emotional, Physical, Financial & Time Reserves You Need**, Navpress, 1992. *Re-establishing margin in our lives – that leeway that once existed between the loads we carry and our limits.*

Taylor, Harold, **Personal Organization**, Time Management Consultants, Inc., 1983. *Step-by-step methods for organizing your work, your environment and yourself.*

Winston, Stephanie, **Best Organizing Tips**, Simon & Schuster, 1995. *Time and space-saving solutions for home and work.*

Winston, Stephanie, **The Organized Executive**, Warner Books, 1983. *A comprehensive look at time and office management.*

Zelinski, Ernie, **The Joy of Not Working**, Visions International Publishing, 1991. *Bringing balance to life by shifting emphasis away from the workplace.*

"A room without books is as

a body without a soul."

Sir John Lubbock

INDEX

Household Hints – Money And Time-Saving Ideas for Home And Garden – Revised Edition – 10% More Hints

Here are useable, useful solutions to everyday cleaning, laundry, cooking, gardening, beauty and health questions.

Retail $12.95 | 144 pages
6" x 9" | 50 line drawings | wire coil bound

Household Hints – Environmental And Energy Hints For Home and Garden

Hundreds of recycling ideas and environmentally friendly alternatives for home and garden, cleaning and maintenance problems. Low-cost, common-sense remedies for everyday problems.

Retail $9.95 | 96 pages
6" x 9" | 40 line drawings | wire coil bound

A Year Of Crafts – For Children And Adults
by Geraldine Hartman

Imaginative craft projects, many with seasonal themes, provide year-round pleasure. Each two-page spread features one child's and one adult's craft with photographs and detailed material and assembly instructions. Suitable for age 6 and up.

Retail $12.95 | 120 pages
6" x 9" | wire coil bound
104 black & white and 32 colored photographs

Cornerstones – An Artist's History Of The City of Regina
by William Argan with Pam Cowan

Historic commercial buildings, schools, churches, hotels, theatres and so much more, Bill Argan's striking illustrations bring the history of Regina alive. Here is a fascinating look at the business, social, political and cultural cornerstones of Regina.

Retail $15.95 | 144 pages
6" x 9" | over 150 illustrations | perfect bound

HomeTips – Organizing Strategies For A Streamlined Home Life
by Patricia Katz

Family and household organizational tips are the focus here. Patricia Katz has created a helpful, humorous and practical guide to help you balance household demands, with family and personal obligations. Take care of the essentials and get more out of life.

Retail $14.95 | 128 pages
6" x 9" | fully illustrated | perfect bound

HELPFUL GIFT IDEAS

WorkTips – *Organizing Strategies For A Productive Work Life* ______x $14.95 = $__________
HomeTips – *Organizing Strategies For A Streamlined Home Life* ____x $14.95 = $__________
Cornerstones – *An Artist's History Of The City of Regina* _________x $15.95 = $__________
Household Hints – *Money & Time-Saving Hints* ________________x $12.95 = $__________
Household Hints – *Environment & Energy Hints* ________________x $9.95 = $__________
A Year of Crafts – *For Children & Adults*_____________________x $12.95 = $__________
Shipping and handling costs ______________________________ = $ 3.00
Subtotal ______________________________ = $__________
In Canada add 7% GST ____________________(Subtotal x .07) = $__________
Total enclosed ______________________________ = $__________

U.S. and international orders payable in U.S. funds/Prices subject to change.

NAME:______________________________
STREET: ______________________________
CITY: ____________________ PROV./STATE ____________________
COUNTRY ____________________ POSTAL/ZIP CODE____________________

Please make cheque or money order payable to:

THE LEADER-POST CARRIER FOUNDATION INC.
P.O. Box 2020
1964 Park Street
Regina, Saskatchewan, Canada S4P 3G4

For fund raising or volume purchase prices, contact
THE LEADER-POST CARRIER FOUNDATION INC. at (306) 565-8240.

HELPFUL GIFT IDEAS

WorkTips – *Organizing Strategies For A Productive Work Life* ______x $14.95 = $__________
HomeTips – *Organizing Strategies For A Streamlined Home Life* ____x $14.95 = $__________
Cornerstones – *An Artist's History Of The City of Regina* _________x $15.95 = $__________
Household Hints – *Money & Time-Saving Hints* ________________x $12.95 = $__________
Household Hints – *Environment & Energy Hints* ________________x $9.95 = $__________
A Year of Crafts – *For Children & Adults*_____________________x $12.95 = $__________
Shipping and handling costs ______________________________ = $ 3.00
Subtotal ______________________________ = $__________
In Canada add 7% GST ____________________(Subtotal x .07) = $__________
Total enclosed ______________________________ = $__________

U.S. and international orders payable in U.S. funds/Prices subject to change.

NAME:______________________________
STREET: ______________________________
CITY: ____________________ PROV./STATE ____________________
COUNTRY ____________________ POSTAL/ZIP CODE____________________

Please make cheque or money order payable to:

THE LEADER-POST CARRIER FOUNDATION INC.
P.O. Box 2020
1964 Park Street
Regina, Saskatchewan, Canada S4P 3G4

For fund raising or volume purchase prices, contact
THE LEADER-POST CARRIER FOUNDATION INC. at (306) 565-8240.